The Ninja
FAQ100

Tsuchiya Haruhito

Sakamoto Mamiko

装 幀 = 寄藤文平、吉田考宏

忍者まるごと事典
The Ninja FAQ100

Tsuchiya Haruhito
土屋晴仁=著

Sakamoto Mamiko
坂本真実子=訳

前書き

⦿日本にも実在した「特別な人たち」

　ある諜報組織のエージェントが、あらゆるテクニックを駆使して敵の中枢部に侵入し、極秘情報を盗んだり、誘拐された味方を救出したり、敵のボスを殺したりして、決定的なダメージを与えるという物語は、昔からたくさんある。映画の『００７』や『ランボー』などのように、何本もシリーズ化されるほどの人気だ。それも虚構の「物語」でなく、リアルなできごとであったりすれば、世界中が注目する。2011年5月の、米国海軍特殊部隊「シールズ」によるウサーマ・ビン・ラーディンの殺害作戦などはその代表的なものだ。

　人々が、このように組織化され訓練された特殊な人々の行動に関心を寄せる理由の第一は、その全貌がなかなか見えない神秘さにある。第二は、彼らがスーパーマンのような能力を身に付けていること。そして第三は、彼らが成し遂げる仕事の大きさにある。

　日本にもそのような「特別な人たち」が存在した。それが忍者である。「忍者」という呼び名や、彼らが用いたテクニックを「忍術」と呼ぶようになるのは、後世になってからであるが、この「特別な人たち」「特別なワザ」については、昔から記録されてきた。しかし、その記録は実に多様であるし、虚実曖昧なものもあるために、本当の姿がどうであったのかはあまりよくわかっていな

Preface

✳ Special People in Ancient Japan

Since ancient times, there have been a lot of tales about a secret agency that managed to get into the center of the enemy camp by any means available and critically damage the enemy by stealing secret information, saving captured comrades or assassinating the enemy's leader. Some of the popular stories about fictional characters like James Bond and Rambo have been made into movie series. However, when the stories are not fictional, the whole world pays even more attention. The military operation by a team of United States Navy SEALs to kill Osama bin Laden is the perfect example of this.

There are several reasons why we are attracted to how such specially trained people are organized and act. Firstly, they are mysterious; secondly, they have special abilities like Superman; and thirdly, they accomplish seemingly impossible tasks.

Such people lived in Japan. It is only fairly recently that they came to be called ninja and their techniques *ninjutsu*, but these special people and their extraordinary techniques have been recorded since olden times. There are a lot of inconsistencies among the materials, and some descriptions seem to be just a mixture of truth and untruth, so their true nature is not clearly

い。ここに想像力の入り込む余地がある。彼らは善人なのか、悪人なのかもはっきりしない。権力者の弾圧に抵抗するゲリラ組織のリーダーだったり、大泥棒だったりする。そのワザについても、空を飛んだり、目の前から一瞬で姿を消したり、水の上を歩くことができたりすると言われた。

21世紀になってから、日本の忍者・忍術に関する研究は急速に進んでいる。たくさん発掘された古文書の解読が進められ、中世の遺跡を調査するなどの学術的なアプローチが生まれている。「伊賀忍者」の故郷にある国立・三重大学人文学部では、2012年に、「忍者」を活かした観光・まちづくりの講演会・シンポジウムを開催して以来、研究の中心地になっている。また忍者・忍術に関する研究書も続々発刊されている。

◉今、起きている「Ninja」ブーム

日本での忍者ブームは過去に何度もあったが、2015年あたりからまた大きなブームが来ている。2015年には、「2月22日」（ニン・ニン・ニン）が、日本記念日協会より「忍者の日」に認定された。同年10月、忍者にゆかりのある日本各地の自治体によって情報交流組織「日本忍者協議会」が発足した。翌2016年7月、ふだんは科学技術に関する展示がメインの日本科学未来館が「The NINJA ―忍者ってナンジャ!?―」という企画展を開催して話題になった。そして2017年10月には、忍者に関する知識を問う「甲賀流忍者検定」（滋賀県・甲賀市観光協会主催）が、10年目にして初めて地元だけでなく東

known. This is where our imagination starts. Were they good guys or bad guys? Some were leaders of rebellious guerrilla groups fighting against authority, and others were master thieves. They were said to have been able to fly in the sky, disappear in an instant or walk on water.

Research on Japanese ninja and *ninjutsu* has been advancing rapidly in this century. Academics have been analyzing numerous ancient documents and carrying out research on medieval ruins. The Faculty of Humanities at Mie University, located in the hometown of the Iga ninja, has been the center of such research since 2012, when they organize seminars and symposia on sightseeing and town development featuring ninja. Academic books on *ninjutsu* have also been published one after another.

❋ The Current Ninja Boom

Japan has had ninja booms many times in the past, and the latest boom started around 2015, when February 22 (in Japanese, *nin, nin, nin*) was recognized as the day of ninja by the Japan Anniversary Association, and in October that year, local governments in places associated with ninja established the Japan Ninja Council to exchange information. In July 2016, the National Museum of Emerging Science and Innovation, whose exhibitions usually relate to science and tech-nology, held a special exhibition "The NINJA—What is a ninja?" that drew widespread attention. Then, in

Preface 7

京でも開催され、200名の応募枠がすぐに埋まるほどの盛況だった。

今回の忍者ブームが、それまでと違うのは、日本よりも早く海外で盛り上がっていた「Ninja」ブームが背景にあることだ。経済産業省が、『クール・ジャパン』ブランドを世界に売り出す取り組みを始めたのは2010年だが、そのアイテムの一つに「Ninja」を取り上げたのも、海外でのブームを受けたからである。もはや「Ninja」は世界のどこでも通じる言葉になっている。その盛り上がり方も一様でないところが面白い。これも、神秘な忍者に対して、それぞれに想像力を働かせた結果だろう。

海外での「Ninja」ブームは、「武術」や「格闘技」に関心を向ける傾向がある。イランでは愛好家約2万4000人のうち、女性(『くノ一』忍者)が3500人もいるが、目的は護身術とエクササイズだという。他には、アニメ『NARUTO』の影響で、忍者のコスチュームやポーズなどを楽しむタイプのブームもある。

◉『Ninja FAQ』の楽しみ方

本書は、日本の忍者に関するFAQ（Frequently Asked Questions）をまとめたガイド本で、全体を6つのカテゴリーに分類している。知りたいところから読むことができる。

できるだけ最新の学術研究の成果も入れたが難しい本

October 2017, the Kōga-Style Ninja Exam (organized by Kōka City Tourism Association in Siga Prefecture) was held in Tokyo as well as in Shiga for the first time in its 10-year history. The number of examinees was limited to 200 people and all the places were soon taken.

The current ninja boom is different from those in the past in that it started overseas first. The Japanese Ministry of Economy, Trade and Industry launched an initiative to spread the "Cool Japan" brand worldwide in 2010, and the ninja was adopted as an export "commodity" in response to this overseas craze. The word ninja has been added to the global vocabulary, and the craze has an interestingly wide variation. This is probably because different people have different conceptions of the mysterious ninja.

Ninja fans abroad tend to have an interest in martial arts and combat sports. In Iran, there are 3,500 women (*kunoichi* ninja) out of 24,000 practitioners, and their primary interest is the art of self-defense and exercise. Other people just like the costumes and poses of ninja due to the influence of the anime *NARUTO*.

✳ About this Book

This book contains FAQs about Japanese ninja and is divided into six parts. Read whatever chapters you like.

The latest study findings have been included whenever possible, but this book is by no means esoteric; it also contains legends and anecdotes that

ではない。昔から、人々の想像力の中で描かれてきた「忍者」の伝説や、物語のバックストーリーも入っている。

　そして忍者についてのおおよその知識が身についたら、伊賀や甲賀などの「聖地」や、全国各地にある「忍者屋敷」のテーマパークに出かけたり、映画やマンガを見直したらもっと楽しくなると思う。大人には、楽しみがいっぱいの「忍者居酒屋」もおすすめだ。

土屋　晴仁

＊謝辞(参考にさせていただいた本やURL)

『忍者の兵法〜三大秘伝書を読む』中島篤巳　角川ソフィア文庫
『忍者の教科書』(2冊) 山田 雄司、伊賀忍者研究会　笠間書院
『忍者の歴史』山田雄司　角川書店
『イラスト図解 忍者』川上仁一
三重大学人文学部「忍者・忍術学講座」
　　http://www.human.mie-u.ac.jp/kenkyu/ken-prj/iga/
　　kouza.html
滋賀県甲賀市観光協会「忍者検定」
　　http://www.koka-kanko.org/contents/ivent/ninja-
　　kentei/ninja-kentei.html
三重県伊賀上野市「伊賀流忍者博物館」
　　http://www.iganinja.jp/museum.html
日本忍者協議会
　　https://ninja-official.com/

reflect the wild imagination of both ancient and contemporary people.

When you have gained a general picture about ninja, you might like to visit some points of interest like Iga and Kōga or the ninja houses that can be found all over the country, or look at movies and comics about ninja. For adults, ninja taverns are also lots of fun!

Tsuchiya Haruhito

目次

前書き Preface 4

Part 1
歴史 History 15

ニンジャはどうして生まれたのか？
Reasons why Ninja Appeared in Japan

Part 2
特技 Special Techniques 39

ニンジャは、こんなことができる
The Ninja's Incredible Abilities

Part 3
道具 Tools 77

ニンジャの武器やコスチューム
Ninja Weapons and Costume

Part 4
思想 Thoughts 111
ニンジャたちの生き方を貫く哲学
Ninja Philosophy, Keeping the Faith

Part 5
伝説 Legends 123
ニンジャのエピソードやレジェンド
Ninja Episodes and Legends

Part 6
研究 Studies 147
ニンジャを学べる資料や"聖地"
Information and Places to Visit

PART 1

歴史
History

ニンジャはどうして生まれたのか？
Reasons why Ninja Appeared in Japan

Q 忍者の先祖はどんな人たちですか？

　はっきりしたことはわかりません。忍者の故郷として有名な三重県・伊賀地方には**5世紀頃の古墳**があり、当時の中国や朝鮮半島からの鉄などの技術を伝えた渡来人の族長が祀られていると言われています。同地の有名な忍者「服部半蔵」の祖先もこの渡来人で**機を織って服**を作っていた人です。

Q 古代にはどんな忍者が活躍したのですか？

　伊賀に伝わる伝承では、神話時代の「神武天皇」が九州から大和征服に向かう際、その先鋒を務め、宮門の警衛も務めた「道臣命」を**伊賀忍者の祖先**としています。

　また伊賀と並んで有名な滋賀県・甲賀地方には、聖徳太子が、587年に**仏教普及**に抵抗する物部氏を征伐した際に、大伴細人というものが活躍し、「しのび（志能便）」と名付けられ、これが「甲賀忍者」の祖になったとの伝承があります。他にも7世紀には「多胡弥」とか、「藤原千方」という忍者が活躍したとの**記録があります**。

Q Who are the ancestors of ninja?

We do not have clear evidence of the origins ninja. Iga (Mie Prefecture), which is famous as one of the homes of ninja, has ancient **burial mounds dating from about the fifth century**. It is said that the heads of the *toraijin* (people from overseas who settled in Japan in the fourth to seventh century), who introduced skills such as making iron tools from China and the Korean Peninsula to Japan during those times, were enshrined in the ancient mounds. The ancestors of Hattori Hanzō, a famous ninja from Iga, were also *toraijin* who **weaved** clothing.

Q Who were some of the important ninja in ancient times?

According to the folktale handed down in Iga, Michi no Omi no Mikoto is the **progenitor of the Iga ninja**. He spearheaded the troops when the legendary Emperor Jimmu headed for Yamato (Nara Prefecture) from the Kyushu region (southwest Japan) to conquer the area, and later guarded the gate of the palace.

Like Iga, Kōga (Shiga Prefecture) is also famous for ninja. In 587, when Prince Shōtoku subjugated the Mononobe clan who had been resisting the **spread of Buddhism**, Ōtomo no Hosohito also exercised his skills as a ninja, and he was later named *shinobi*.* Another folktale says that he became the ancestor of the

---

Shinobi literally means "hide." In the native (*kun'yomi*) kanji reading, it is pronounced *shinobi* (shortened from *shinobi no mono*). Ninja is an alternative (*on'yomi*) reading.

History 17

Q　「伊賀」と「甲賀」はなぜ有名なのですか？

　三重県北部の「伊賀」と滋賀県南部の「甲賀」は隣り合った集落で、昔から交流がありました。共通しているのは、①京都に近いので情報が伝わりやすいこと、②都で戦乱があると**雑役の仕事を請負っていた**こと、③**周辺の有力豪族**から自治を認められていたことがあげられます。雑役といっても情報収集と**敵陣をかく乱する**術を活かした特殊技能です。このレベルが高いことが広く認められ、各地の有力武将に雇われたことが「伊賀」「甲賀」を有名にしました。伊賀と甲賀は互いに**防衛同盟**を結んでいました。

Q　「伊賀」と「甲賀」はどう違うのですか？

伊賀甲賀の位置

　今は三重県と滋賀県に分かれていますが、昔は境を意識せずに雑居していました。場所を説明するのに「伊賀の甲賀」と言ったり、「甲伊一国」という言い方もしました。同盟関係だった両者が**一時期敵対**したのは織田信長の第2

18　歴史

Kōga ninja. **In the written record**, other ninja called Takoya and Fujiwara no Chikata were also active in the seventh century.

Q Why are Iga and Kōga famous for ninja?

Iga (in the northern part of Mie Prefecture) and Kōga (in the southern part of Shiga Prefecture) are adjacent provinces and mingled with each other for a long time. The two areas had common features: 1) they were able to obtain information easily because of their proximity to Kyoto, 2) they **undertook fatigue duties** during conflicts and wars in Kyoto, and 3) they were given the status of self-governing body by **nearby powerful clans**. The fatigue duties required special techniques for collecting information and **disrupting the enemy's camps**. Their expertise became widely recognized and ninja were hired by powerful warlords in various parts of Japan, which made the two provinces famous. They formed a **defense alliance** with each other.

Q What is the difference between Iga and Kōga?

Nowadays, Iga and Kōga belong to different prefectures, Mie Prefecture and Shiga Prefecture, respectively. However, the two areas existed together without borders in ancient times. When explaining their location, they were said to be Iga no Kōga (Kōga of Iga) or *kōi ikkoku* (Kōga and Iga are one province). It was at the time of the second attack on Iga by Oda Nobunaga (in 1581) that these two areas that had built an alliance were **temporarily hostile** toward each other and Kōga

次伊賀攻め（1581年）で、甲賀側が信長につきました。しかし後にはまた共存もしています。「伊賀流」「甲賀流」とそれぞれが**ブランド力を競う**ようになったのは後世になってからです。

Q 忍者が活躍した昔の戦いを教えてください

14世紀の鎌倉時代から室町時代にかけての記録があります。たとえば**鎌倉幕府打倒**を呼びかけた後醍醐天皇に味方した楠木正成は、1333年、千早・赤阪城でわずか1000人で、100万にも及ぶ鎌倉幕府の大軍を**ゲリラ戦**で撃破しました。

この時、伊賀・服部氏の忍者48名が大活躍しました。また、日本が**戦国時代**に入った15世紀後半の1487年、足利将軍の幕府軍が、反抗する近江の土豪・六角氏を攻めた際には、伊賀と甲賀の忍者たちが**敵陣に放火する**などして、幕府軍を追い返しました。

took Nobunaga's side. After that, however, Iga and Kōga coexisted alongside one other once again. It was not until later that the Iga-ryū (the Iga School of *ninjutsu*) and the Kōga-ryū (the Kōga School) **competed for their supremacy**.

Q Please tell us about the wars in which ninja served vigorously in ancient times.

There are several written records about the wars that took place from the Kamakura period to the Muromachi period in the 14th century. For instance, when Emperor Godaigo called for **overthrowing the Kamakura shogunate**, Kusunoki Masashige took the Emperor's side. In 1333, besieged in Chihaya and Akasaka Castles (Osaka Prefecture), he and his 1,000 combatants employed **guerilla tactics** and managed to defeat as many as one million soldiers of the shogunate.

At that time, 48 ninja of the Hattori clan in Iga served vigorously in the war. In 1487, at the beginning of the **Warring States period** in Japan, the army led by the shogun Ashikaga Yoshihisa attacked the Rokkaku clan in Ōmi (Shiga Prefecture) who opposed the shogunate. During the conflict, ninja from Iga and Kōga beat off the shogunate army by **setting fire to the enemy's camp**.

Q 「忍者」という名前は昔からありましたか？

　「忍者」という言葉はありましたが、**一般的ではなく**、「忍び（の者）」とか「草」と呼ばれました。「忍者」という統一した名前が定着したのは近世になってからです。各地では、それぞれの名前で呼ばれていました。

　藩主直轄の集団には特別な名前もありました。奥羽では「草」、相模の「風魔」、「北条乱波」、甲州の「三つ者」、「透波」、越後の「軒猿」、加賀の「偸組」、伊達の「黒脛巾組」などと呼ばれました。

Q 「忍者」は全国にいたのですが？

　物語などでよく知られているのは、信濃（長野県）で真田幸村が率いた「真田十勇士」や戸隠忍者、**鉄砲を特技とした**紀州（和歌山県）の雑賀衆・根来衆があります。

　先のQ&Aでも紹介した以外にも、出羽（秋田・山形県）の羽黒忍者、安芸（広島県）の福島忍者などが伝わっています。現在、こうした忍者ゆかりの自治体は、「日本忍者協議会」という交流組織を作っています。

Q Was the word ninja used in ancient times?

The word ninja did exist, but it was **not in common use**. Ninja were called *shinobi no mono* (hiding person) or *kusa* (grass). The word ninja became a fixed and standardized name only after the early modern period. There was a variety of different names to describe ninja in different regions.

Also, ninja groups that were directly **controlled by feudal lords** were given special names. Some examples include *kusa* in Ōu (Tohoku), *fūma* and *hōjo-rappa* in Sagami (Kanagawa), *mitsumono* and *suppa* in Kōshū (Yamanashi), *nokizaru* in Echigo (Niigata), *nusumigumi* in Kaga (Ishikawa), and *kurohabakigumi* (founded by the Date clan in Sendai).

Q Did ninja exist in the whole of Japan?

Some of the legendary ninja are Sanada-Jūyūshi (the Ten Heroes of Sanada) led by Sanada Yukimura and Togakushi ninja in Shinano (Nagano Prefecture), as well as Saiga shū and Negoro shū in Kishū (Wakayama Prefecture), who **were experts with guns**.

In addition, the names of other ninja such as Haguro ninja in Dewa (Akita and Yamagata Prefectures) and Fukushima ninja in Aki (Hiroshima Prefecture) have been passed down the generations. Recently, local governments in connection with ninja have established an organization for cultural exchange called the Japan Ninja Council.

Q 織田信長はなぜ伊賀を滅ぼしたのですか？

　国内統一を進めたい織田信長にとって、京都への道を塞ぐ位置にあり、住人たちの自治で治めている伊賀の国は邪魔でした。

　1579年、織田信長の次男・信雄（のぶかつ）が攻め入ったが伊賀者のゲリラ戦術に敗退。1581年、信長自身が4万人以上の軍勢を率いて侵攻。**女も子どもも殺戮する徹底した殲滅作戦**で、伊賀は敗北しました。

　この戦いを「天正伊賀の乱」と呼び、2017年夏公開の映画『忍びの国』ほか、たくさんの映画や小説に取り上げられています。

Q 秀吉の「中国大返し」にも忍者は関係していますか？

　明智光秀が京都・本能寺で信長を襲った1582年6月、羽柴秀吉は、**信長の武将として**中国地方の毛利を攻め、陣中では厳しい警戒体制を敷いていました。その警戒網にひっかかったのは、明智側の忍者・藤田伝八郎でした。伝八郎は盲人を装い無関係を装ったのですが、毛利宛に内通すると書いた**密書**を隠していたのがばれてその場で処刑。信長の死を毛利より早く察知した秀吉は、すぐに**和議を結んで**、中国地方から驚異的な速度で東へ引き返し、明智を討ったのです。これが「中国大返し」です。

Q Why did Oda Nobunaga destroy Iga?

Iga Province (Mie Prefecture) was an obstruction to Nobunaga who wanted to **unify the country**, because it was situated in a location that blocked the way to Kyoto and the residents themselves governed the region.

In 1579, his second son Nobukatsu attempted to attack Iga, but was defeated by the guerrilla tactics of Iga ninja. In 1581, Nobunaga launched his own invasion of Iga by leading troops consisting of more than 40,000 soldiers. Iga was defeated by the complete **annihilation strategy of including the slaughter of women and children**.

This war is called the *Tenshō Iga no ran*. The war has been depicted in the film titled "MUMON: The Land of Stealth," which was released in the summer of 2017, as well as in many other films and novels.

Q Did ninja relate to *chūgoku ōgaeshi* by Hideyoshi?

In June 1582, Akechi Mitsuhide assassinated Oda Nobunaga at Honnōji Temple in Kyoto. At that time, Hashiba Hideyoshi was fighting against the Mōri clan in the Chūgoku region **as a vassal of Oda**. On heightened state of alert, Hashiba's soldiers caught Fujita Dempachirō, a ninja hired by Akechi. Fujita pretended to be blind and have no connection with Akechi, but they discovered that he had hidden his master's **confidential letter** to the Mōri clan with the aim of seeking conspiracy. He was executed on the spot. Thus Hideyoshi managed to know Nobunaga's death earlier

Q 忍者が徳川家康を助けたのは本当ですか？

本当です。前のQ&Aで紹介した本能寺の変の時、徳川家康は大阪・堺に滞在していました。家康は**信長の盟友**だったので自分も狙われることになります。知らせを聞いて、すぐに伊賀の山道を逃げ、「鹿伏兎(かぶと)」の険も越えて本拠・岡崎に帰りました。途中まで同行して別の道を逃げた穴山梅雪(あなやまばいせつ)は、**落ち武者狩り**の土民に殺されました。この伊賀越えには、家康の部下・服部半蔵(はっとりはんぞう)が声をかけて、伊賀と甲賀の忍者が集まって助けました。後に、数百人が家康に召し抱えられ半蔵の部下に配属されました。

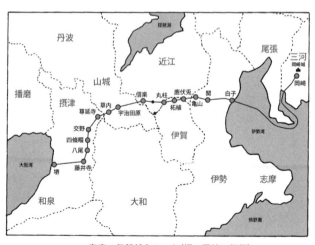

家康の伊賀越えルート(堺〜岡崎の行程)

than the Mōri clan. He quickly **made peace** with his opponent, returned eastward from the Chūgoku area at a phenomenal speed, and defeated Akechi. This series of military action is called *chūgoku ōgaeshi*.

Q Is it true that ninja helped Tokugawa Ieyasu?

True. When the Honnōji incident mentioned in the previous Q&A occurred, Tokugawa Ieyasu was staying in Sakai, Osaka. As he was **Nobunaga's sworn friend**, he was also in danger of assassination. As soon as he heard about the incident, he escaped through the mountain paths of Iga, crossed the dangerous pass called *Kabuto*, and returned to his home, Okazaki. On the other hand, Anayama Baisetsu, who went with Ieyasu part of the way but later escaped separately from Ieyasu, was killed by local in habitants who were **hunting fleeing defeated warriors**. At the time of this crossing of Iga, Hattori Hanzō, who was the Ieyasu's vassal, asked the ninja of Iga and Kōga to help Ieyasu. Later, several hundred ninja were employed by Ieyasu and became Hanzō's subordinates.

Q 東京の地名にある「半蔵門」はどんないわれがありますか？

家康に重用された服部半蔵とその部下は、江戸城西門の警備を任されました。皇居の西側にある「半蔵門」がそれで、反対の東側が正面玄関の大手門です。

門内は、江戸時代には吹上御庭と呼ばれ、**隠居した先代将軍**や、**将軍継嗣**などの住居とされました。半蔵門からまっすぐ西に延びる道路は甲州街道（現・国道20号）に通じており、いざという時には、**幕府の天領**である甲府へと安全に避難するための重要な道でした。

Q 忍者を外国人が知るようになったのはいつからですか？

徳川家康が将軍になって「江戸幕府」を開いた1603年に、ポルトガル語による日本語の辞書『日葡辞書』が長崎で印刷されました。これは日本に来ていた**イエズス会の宣教師**たちが4年かけて作成したものです。そこには「Xinobi（シノビ）」の項目があり、「戦争の際に、状況を探るために、夜、または、こっそりと隠れて城内へよじ上ったり陣営内に入ったりする**間諜**」との解説があります。戦国時代の活躍が広く知られていたことがわかります。

Q What story lies behind the place-name *Hanzōmon* in Tokyo?

Hattori Hanzō, who **was given an important position by Ieyasu**, and his subordinates were responsible for guarding the west gate of Edo Castle. The gate is called *Hanzōmon* (Hanzō Gate) and is now situated on the west side of the Imperial Palace. On the east side, opposite to *Hanzōmon*, is *Ōtemon* (the front gate).

During the Edo period, the vast area inside of the *Hanzōmon* gate was called *Fukiage oniwa* (Fukiage garden), where houses for **retired previous shoguns** or **shoguns' heirs** dotted. The road that extends straight toward the west leads to the Kōshū Kaidō (now National Route 20). Therefore, in an emergency, the road was important as an escape route to Kōfu (located in Yamanashi Prefecture), which was the **shogunal demesne**.

Q How long have foreigners known about ninja?

In 1603, when Tokugawa Ieyasu became a shogun and established the Edo shogunate, Nippo jisho (Japanese–Portuguese dictionary) was published in Nagasaki. It was compiled by **Jesuit missionaries** who stayed in Japan and the task lasted four years. Interestingly, it has an entry for *xinobi* (shinobi). According to the dictionary, a *xinobi* is a **spy** who climbs up the walls of castles and infiltrates into camps at night or secretly to collect information. This shows that the ninja's activities during the Warring States period were widely known.

Q キリシタンが反乱した「島原（天草）の乱」ではどうでしたか？

　「島原（天草）の乱」の最後は山上の「原城」の攻防戦でした。この時、松平信綱配下の甲賀忍者10名が活躍。彼らは城内に潜入して**諜報活動を行ったり、兵糧攻め**にあえぐ城内から米俵を盗み出したりしました！　「忍者」が実際の大きな戦争に参加した記録はこれが最後でした。

Q 「忠臣蔵」の名場面「赤穂城明け渡し」と忍者の関係は？

　赤穂城主・浅野内匠頭は江戸城「松の廊下」で吉良上野介に斬りかかって（1701年）、切腹になりました。

　国元の赤穂藩家老・大石内蔵助は、**武装抵抗せず**平和裏に城を幕府に明け渡しました。この間の動静がどうなるか、一番心配したのは隣接する岡山藩で、すぐに忍者を忍び込ませて、赤穂城内の議論の様子を細かく調べさせたのです。

Q **How did ninja act during the Shimabara (Amakusa) rebellion when Christians rose up in revolt?**

The Shimabara (Amakusa) rebellion came to an end in the battle at Hara Castle on the mountain. At that time, ten Kōga ninja led by Matsudaira Nobutsuna served outstandingly against the rebels. They infiltrated the castle, **carried out espionage** and stole bags of rice from the castle where people were struggling against **starvation tactics**. These accounts are the last record of ninja taking part in a major war.

Q **What relations do ninja have with the evacuation of Akō Castle?**

In 1701, the lord of Akō Castle, Asano Takumi no Kami, wounded Kira Kōzukenosuke in *matsu no rōka* (the corridor of pine trees) in Edo Castle and then he was commanded to commit *hara-kiri* (suicide by disembowelment).

After a heated debate among vassals, Ōishi Kuranosuke, the head of chief retainers in the Akō Domain, decided to evacuate the castle peacefully **without armed resistance** against the shogunate. Having been worried the most about the situation in the castle, the neighboring Okayama Domain sent ninja to infiltrate into the castle and investigate how the debate went on in the castle.

Q 「お庭番」というのも忍者ですか？

　正体もはっきりしている武士なので、忍者というより警護役兼探索役です。紀州（和歌山）の藩主から将軍になった8代将軍の徳川吉宗が、紀州から呼び寄せた側近の武士から17家の者を選びました。元は戦場で大将の銃に火薬を詰める任務でした。

　江戸市中だけでなく蝦夷（北海道）の探索にも出かけています。彼らは、いつも「**丸に十字型**」の紋が入った小紋を着ていました。

Q 平和な江戸時代にも忍者はいましたか？

　はい、いました。江戸幕府は、諸藩の動向に常に警戒を怠りませんでしたから、情報収集のために各国に「隠密」を送り込んでいました。これは諸国の藩も同様でしたから、互いに隠密を警戒していたのです。隠密は見つかればその場ですぐに切られても止むを得ないと思われていました。

Q Was *oniwaban* also a ninja?

Since *oniwaban* was a **samurai with a clear identity**, he was not a ninja but rather a person who served as a guard and espionage. The eighth shogun Tokugawa Yoshimune, who became a shogun after being the feudal lord of the Kishū Domain (Wakayama Prefecture), appointed warriors from 17 families from Kishū to *oniwaban*. Their original job in Kishū had been to load the generals' guns with powder on the battlefield.

They went to explore Edo as well as Ezo (Hokkaido). They always wore *komon* (fine pattern on kimono materials) with a *mon* (family crest) of a **cross in a circle**.

Q Did ninja exist during the peaceful Edo period?

Yes, they did. As the Edo shogunate never stopped watching the situation of domains closely, *onmitsu* were sent to provinces to collect information. Domains also sent *onmitsu*, so both sides kept an eye out for each other's *onmitsu*. *Onmitsu* were unable to escape being executed on the spot as soon as they were revealed.

Q 幕末の19世紀にも忍者が活躍したというのは本当ですか？

幕末になると、日本は幕府を助けるか倒すかで国論が二分されました。幕府は討幕派の中心・長州藩（山口県）にたくさんの忍者を送り、長州支藩の岩国伊賀忍者から情報を聞き出しました。

奇兵隊や高杉晋作の動向、英国軍艦の様子もすべて調べていました。一方の長州も、幕府の動向を調べるなど、両方の諜報合戦が盛んでした。結果として負けたのは幕府軍でした。

Q 20世紀にも忍者はいましたか？

忍者の後継者と名乗る人はたくさんいます。日本陸軍のスパイ養成所であった「陸軍中野学校」で忍術の講義をした藤田西湖は甲賀流忍術14世を名乗り、多方面に異色の才能を発揮しました。

東日教は、伊賀流24代を名乗り、数々の"忍術"を披露しました。現存する人では、9つの忍術流派を継承し、広く海外で格闘や護身術と礼

Q **Is it true that ninja also played important roles in the closing days of the Tokugawa shogunate in the 19th century?**

In the end of Tokugawa shogunate, public opinion in Japan was divided into whether to support or to overthrow the shogunate. The shogunate sent a number of ninja to the Chōshū Domain (Yamaguchi Prefecture), which was the center of the **anti-shogunate faction**, and they gathered information in Iwakuni Domain, the branch domain of Chōshū.

The shogunate also found out all the movements of the **Irregular Militia** (*Kiheitai*) and Takasugi Shinsaku, and the situation of British warships. Meanwhile, the Chōshū Domain was also careful with the development in the shogunate, and the espionage battle between the shogunate and the opposition force was fierce. In the end, the shogunate army was defeated.

Q **Did ninja exist in the 20th century?**

A number of people have **described themselves as successors of ninja**. Fujita Seiko announced himself as the 14th master of the Kōga-ryū (Kōga School) of *ninjutsu* (ninja techniques) and taught it at Rikugun Nakano Gakkō (the Army School in Nakano), a training school for spies in the Japanese army. He displayed his unique talents in a wide range of fields.

Azuma Nikkyō named himself the 24th head of Iga-ryū (Iga School) and demonstrated numerous *ninjutsu* skills. Among the living, Hatsumi Masaaki

History 35

儀を教えている初見良昭が有名。また甲賀流を継承した川上仁一は、総合サバイバル術を教え、著書もあり、三重大学特任教授になるなど忍者研究者としても活躍しています。

is one of the most famous; he inherited nine schools of *ninjutsu* and is teaching hand-to-hand martial arts, **the art of self-defense** and manners in various foreign countries. Further, Kawakami Jin'ichi, who inherited Kōga-ryū, teaches general survival techniques and has written some books. He has also been appointed a professor at Mie University as a researcher on ninja.

PART 2

特技
Special Techniques

ニンジャは、こんなことができる
The Ninja's Incredible Abilities

Q 水面を歩くことができたのは本当ですか？

体を濡らさずに**城の周囲にある堀**などを渡る際には、足に履く円盤状の板「水蜘蛛」を用いたと言われます。でもこれで体重を支えるのは無理なので、高く張った綱をつかみながら進んだとか、もっと大きな板にまたがってサーフボードのパドリングのように進んだ、浮き輪を使ったなどと言われています。少年向けのマンガ『サスケ』では、長いムシロを浮かべて、沈まないうちに高速で走り渡る方法が描かれていますが、実際には無理でしょう。

[水搔]

Q 忍者は空を飛べましたか？

これは明らかに無理でしょう。忍者小説などには凧にのって城の**天守閣に降りた**という話や、布や傘をパラシュートのように使って空から舞い降りたという話が出てきますが、物理的には無理です。

ただ、鍛えぬいた体を敏捷に動かすことができたはずですから、高く張り巡らしたロープを伝ったり、**木の枝を飛び移ったり**、高いところから飛び降りてもケガなく着地することはできたでしょう。それがあたかも空を飛ぶように見えたのかもしれません。

Q Is it true that ninja could walk on water?

Some people say ninja used *mizugumo* (a water-crossing device, literally a water spider). The *mizugumo* was a disc-shaped board that ninja attached to their feet in order to cross **a moat surrounding a castle** without getting wet. However, the buoyancy of this device would have been too poor to bear their weight. So others say that ninja advanced while holding ropes stretched in the air, moved forward on a bigger board like paddling on the surfboard, or used a flotation ring. *Sasuke*, a cartoon aimed at young male audiences, depicts a method of crossing water by running rapidly over long straw mats floating on the water to thus avoid sinking. However, in fact, it is impossible to do this.

Q Could ninja fly in the sky?

Clearly impossible. Books such as ninja novels include stories of **landing on a castle tower** by flying in the air using a kite or descending down from the sky using a piece of cloth or an umbrella like a parachute. However, this would have been physically impossible.

Instead, it is thought that ninja were extremely agile and simply moved their well-trained physique in such a way that they could land without any injury even if they moved along ropes stretched up high, **leapt from branch to branch** among trees or jumped down from a high place. Those actions might have made it look as if they were flying in the sky.

Q 「火遁の術」、「土遁の術」はどんなものですか？

「遁」とは逃げる意味です。火の中で燃えたように見せて逃げる「火遁の術」では、火薬を使って大きな炎を作り、赤い布を投げて炎から抜け出したように見せかけます。実際には穴を掘って石綿でできた布で身を守りました。

「土遁の術」も同じように**用意してあった穴の中に隠れ**、表面を土や木の葉で覆って擬装しました。他にも目立たない色の布で壁や木々の間に隠れてカモフラージュしたと言われます。

くりぬいた竹の筒を使って水中で呼吸しながら身を隠す「水遁の術」もあります。でも、ほとんどマンガのネタです。

Q 忍者が術を使う前に、独特の形に手を組むのはなぜですか？

独特の手や指の形に組むことを**密教**では「印を結ぶ」といいます。たとえば、至高の存在である「大日如来」の印の一つは左手の人差し指を立て、その人差し指を右手で包み込む「智拳印」です。

42 ✦ 特技

Q What are *katon no jutsu* (Fire technique) and *doton no jutsu* (Earth technique)?

Ton means to escape. One of the methods of escape that ninja used was *katon no jutsu* in which it looked like ninja are burning alive in a fire. By setting a big fire with gunpowder and throwing red cloths in the air, it looked as if they had escaped. In fact, they dug holes in which to hide and protected themselves using fabric made of asbestos.

Doton no jutsu refers to the technique of **hiding in caves that they had already prepared**, in the same way as *katon no jutsu*, and disguising themselves by covering themselves with soil or the leaves of trees. In addition, it is said that they hid in front of the walls or between trees by wearing inconspicuously colored clothes and thus camouflaging themselves.

There is also *suiton no jutsu* in which they hid themselves under water while **breathing through hollow bamboo tubes**. However, almost all these stories are cartoon-like fiction.

Q Why did ninja make a special shape by crossing their fingers and hands before using *ninjutsu*?

The making of a special shape by crossing the fingers and hands is known as *in wo musubu* (to make symbolic signs with fingers) in **esoteric Buddhism**. For example, *chiken-in* (the knowledge-fist mudra) involves stretching the forefinger of the left hand and wrapping the finger with the right hand, which is one of the mudras of Dainichi Nyorai (Vairocana) and signifies supreme existence.

これで呪力を授かり、姿を消したり、嵐を起こしたりするというのは無理ですが、精神集中に大きな効果がありました。

九字印

※九字印は臨、兵、闘、者、皆、陣、烈、在、前の順番に印を結んでいく

臨 独鈷印

人差し指を前に出す。護身としての意味がある

兵 大金剛輪印

中指を人差し指の上に絡める。滅罪を表す

闘 外獅子印

中指を人差し指に絡める。魔よけ効果がある。

者 内獅子印

左右の中指を薬指に絡める。悪を退かせる

皆 外縛印

両手の指を外側に組んで、拳の形を作る

陣 内縛印

両指のすべてを内側に入れて手を組む

烈 智拳印

左手の人差し指を立て、右手を重ねる

在 日輪印

左右の手を大きく広げて前に突き出す

前 隠形印

左手の拳を右手のひらのうえに置く。姿を隠す意味

Although it was impossible for ninja to **be blessed with magical powers**, to disappear and to cause storms by using this gesture, the mudra had a great effect in terms of concentration of the mind.

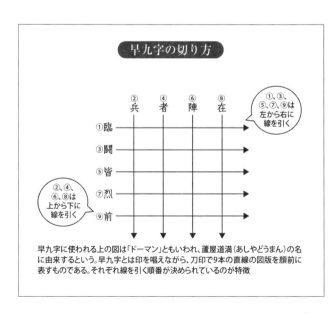

他にも、修験道の影響を受けた「九字の印」が有名で、「臨・兵・闘・者・皆・陳・裂・在・前」の**九字を唱えながら**、両手で9通りの「印」を結びます。これで自分の周囲に結界（バリアー）を作り、**邪気**が入り込まないようにしました。

Q 忍者が「巻き物」をくわえている絵がありますが？

それは江戸時代の創作で、**巻き物をくわえて**印を結ぶと、消えたり、怪物になったりする芝居が受けました。この「巻き物」は、忍術の奥義を書き記したもので、これを持っていることは、「一子相伝」（跡継ぎの一人にだけ伝える）で強力な秘密の技をマスターしたという想定です。

この巻き物を「虎の巻」と呼ぶのは、**中国の兵法書**「六韜」で奥義を書いたのが「虎の巻」だったからです。現代では教科書の解説本、受験用ガイドブックの意味で使われますね。

46 ✚ 特技

Another famous mudra is *kuji no in* (the mudra of nine symbols), which is derived from *shugendō* (mountain asceticism). *Kuji no in* is created from nine kinds of gesture using both hands **while chanting nine symbols**: *Rin* (Power), *Hyō* (Energy), *Tō* (Harmony), *Sha* (Healing), *Kai* (Intuition), *Chin* (Awareness), *Retsu* (Dimension), *Zai* (Creation), and *Zen* (Absolute). These gestures are said to have helped the ninja to bond with the sacred space around them and keep out **noxious vapors**.

Q Pictures exist that depict ninja with scrolls in their mouth.

These pictures are a creation of the Edo period. At that time, in plays, ninja disappeared and became monsters after putting **a scroll in their mouth** and making symbolic signs with their fingers. This was a very popular idea among the people of that period. It was believed that the secret techniques of *ninjutsu* were written on this scroll. Thus it was assumed that possessing this scroll meant that the person had mastered powerful secret techniques through *Isshisōden* (transmission from a father to one of his offspring).

This scroll was called *tora no maki* (literally, the volume of the tiger) because in a **Chinese treatise on military strategy** titled *Rikutō* ("The six secret techniques"), some secret techniques were disclosed in the volume called *tora no maki*. In modern times, the phrase *tora no maki* means study-aid books for textbooks and exams.

Q 「抜き足、差し足、忍び足」とは?

敵の家の中を、音を立てずに歩くのは忍術の基本。地面につけた足をかかとから静かに上げる(抜き足)、上げた足を小指の指先から静かに下ろす(差し足)を繰り返す歩き方が「忍び足」です。

ほかにも「**歩き方十か条**」があり、体をかがませて、床についた両手の上に足を乗せて進む方法や、逃走用に撒いた「蒔きビシ」を自分で踏まないように「すり足」で歩く方法、和服の厚い帯を敷いて特別な草履で歩く方法などが伝えられています。また忍者志望者の採用に、くしゃくしゃにした紙をばらまいた部屋の中を、音を立てずに歩く試験がありました。

深草兎歩

体を丸めてなるべく姿勢を低く保つようにする

足を手の上に乗せる

手の上に足をのせて歩く方法。音を出しにくくする。敵の侵入を知らせるために作られたウグイス張りの床や草むらなどでその効力を発したという。

Q What do *nuki-ashi, sashi-ashi* and *shinobi-ashi* mean?

Walking without making a noise in the enemy's house is a basic ninja technique. *Nuki-ashi* means to raise the feet silently by pulling them up from the ground from the heels first. *Sashi-ashi* means to put the feet silently onto the ground by putting the fifth toe first. The walking style that involves repeating those actions is called *shinobi-ashi*.

Ninja also had **ten basic walking methods**. For example, they used a way of moving forward that involved bending down, putting their hands on the floor, and then putting their feet on their hands. They also used *suri-ashi* (moving the feet without raising them off the ground) so as not to tread on traps like *makibishi* (spiked devices scattered on the ground to maim infantry, literally caltrop), which they scattered to aid in their escape. There were also ways of walking in special *zōri* (Japanese sandals) that were made of the thick *obi* (the belt) of kimono. A test was used before employing ninja and to assess ninja-to-be that examined whether they could walk without making any noise in a room in which lots of crumpled pieces of paper were scattered on the floor.

Q 忍者は「格闘技」の達人でしたか？

もちろん。ふだんから肉体を鍛え、剣術、柔術、棒術を磨いていました。また手近なものを武器にして戦う知恵にも優れていました。それらはみな「一子相伝」で秘密ですが、格闘術として柔術を伝えた流派も少しあったようです。現在、世界での「Ninja」ブームはこの武術が強調され、護身術として教えている「道場」もあります。しかし忍者は、戦って勝つよりも生きて情報を持ち返ることが一番優先されたので、戦う場合でも、攻撃をかわしながら逃走する方法を考えていました。

Q 石垣を登ったり塀を越える時の術は？

はしごを用意できるなら一番簡単ですが、音がしないように、はしごの上下左右の四隅に布を巻き付けて、音を立てないようにしました。また鉄製の碇のような金属を先端につけた「鍵縄」を投げ上げてひっかけ、石の間に足がか

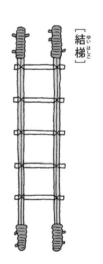

［結梯（ゆいはしご）］

Q Were ninja the masters of martial arts?

Of course, ninja were the masters of martial arts. They usually trained their body and improved their skills in *kenjutsu* (the Japanese swordsmanship), *jūjutsu* (the art of close combat with a short weapon or no weapon at all), and *bōjutsu* (the art of using a stick as a weapon). They also had superior wisdom in being able to fight using familiar tools as weapons. Although all the information was secret because of *isshisōden*, there seem to have been some schools of *ninjutsu* that introduced *jūjutsu* as a martial arts technique. Recently, a ninja boom around the world has resulted in an emphasis on this martial art and some *dōjō* (a training place for martial arts) in Japan are teaching *ninjutsu* as a method of self-defense. However, for ninja the highest priority tasks were to stay alive and to return with information rather than to defeat their enemies. Thus, in a battle, they were always thinking about how to escape while parrying their opponents' attacks.

Q What technique did ninja use when climbing up stone walls or climbing over fences?

The easiest way for ninja to do this was to use ladders if they could prepare in advance. Ninja tried not to make any noise by wrapping cloth around the four ends of the ladder. Furthermore, they climbed up walls by throwing up a *kaginawa* (grappling hook) made of iron like an anchor that was attached to the end of a rope, hooking it over the top of the wall, and driving in wedges between stones to create footholds. Also, by

りになるクサビを差し込みながら登ります。また、塀に立てかけた**刀の鍔**を足がかりにする時は、刀の「**下げ緒**」を足首に結んでのぼり、塀の上から刀を引き上げます。

基本はクライミングと同じで、筋力、とくに指先は、砂や石を詰めた器に突っ込んで鍛えました。

Q 高いところから降りる時にはどうしましたか?

子どもたちが「忍者ごっこ」をしてケガをする原因の一つがこれです。着地する時に膝を曲げ、前転すれば衝撃がやわらぎますが、慣れる必要があります。書物には、「竹竿や紐に伝いながら背中を崖や壁側につけてこするようして降りるとよい」、「近くに木が生えていればそれに飛び移ってから降りる」など、少しでも安全になる方法が書かれています。

Q 狭いところを関節をはずして通り抜けたのは本当ですか?

建物の狭い隙間を抜けるのに、ひじや肩の関節を自由にはずせると便利です。これを得意とした忍者もいたようですし、後に忍者の見世物で実演もされました。でもすべての忍者が「**関節はずし**」をしていた記録はありません。

standing **the guard of a sword** up against the fence as a foothold, they could climb up it and by fastening the **sword strap** around their ankle they could pull up the sword when they got to the top of the fence. Basically, ninja required the same physical strength as climbers. In particular, they improved the strength of the tips of their fingers pummeling sand or stones in containers.

Q How did ninja jump down from a high point?

One of the reasons why children have been injured in *ninja gokko* (childhood ninja games) is that ninja often jumped down from high places. If people bend their knees and roll forward when landing, the impact can be reduced, but they have to get used to doing so. Some documents show safer ways of jumping. For instance, it is written that "When you jump down, you should keep your back to the precipice or wall while holding a bamboo pole or a cord" and "If you find a tree near you, you should climb down after flying to the branch of the tree."

Q Is it true that ninja passed through narrow places by dislocating their joints?

It was convenient for ninja to be able to dislocate their elbow joints and their shoulders at any time in order to get through narrow spaces between buildings. There seem to have been ninja who were good at this technique. Later, this skill was performed in ninja shows. However, no written records have been found that confirm that all ninja **dislocated their joints**.

Special Techniques 53

Q 忍者は「測量」の名人だったのですか？

そうです。決まった長さごとに縛り目を結んだ縄は**必需品**でした。また自分の歩幅を単位に距離を測ったり、今の「**三角測量**」**の原理**を使って城壁の高さを測ったりもしました。三角測量のやり方は、適当な長さの真っ直ぐな枝に目盛りをつけ、腕を真っ直ぐに伸ばして対象と自分との距離と、枝の目盛りからその高さを割り出したのです。

今の三角関数のやり方なら、角度 $A = \theta$ に対して三角形の辺の比 $h : a$（対象の高さ）$: b$（対象との距離）が決まることから、$\sin \theta = a/h$ で、わかりますね。

Q **夜でも方角や時間までわかったのはどんな方法でしたか？**

星、とくに**北斗七星**（別名：北辰、破軍星）を見定めました。杓の2つの星（ドゥーベとメラク）を5倍伸ばしたところにあるのが、ほとんど動かない北極星です。そちらが北で、右手側が東、左手側が西、背中側が南になります。

Q Were ninja experts in measurement?

Yes, they were. A rope along which knots were made at intervals of a certain length was a **requisite** for ninja. In addition, ninja measured distance in units equal to the length of their steps and also measured the height of ramparts based on what we now know as the **principle of triangulation**. For triangulation, first they drew a line on a straight branch, which had a certain length, then they marked another line on the branch which was measured by stretching their arms, and lastly they calculated the height of the object by the distance between the object and themselves, and the length of the marked line on the branch.

If we use the present-day trigonometric function, the ratio h of the height of the object (a): the distance from the object (b) is determined when an angle (θ) of a triangle is given, and then the formula $\sin \theta = a/h$ can be applied.

Q How did ninja get directions and the time even at night?

Ninja located the position of the stars, especially the **Big Dipper** (Ursa Major, also known as *hokushin or hagunsei*). Polaris hardly moves and is located by extending a line five times longer through the front two stars, Dubhe (α) and Merak (β) of the ladle. If you look up at Polaris, the direction in which you are looking is north, the right-hand side of the star is east, the left-hand side is west, and the direction behind your is south.

北斗七星は一日で北極星の周り360度を回ります。ということは、1時間なら15度、2時間で30度。これほど大きく動くので季節ごとのだいたいの時間が分かったのです。他にも28の星座（「28宿」）を知って方角の目安にしました。

Q 忍者の「観察力」とはどんなものですか？

知らない土地で行動するには観察力が重要でした。忍者はどこへ行っても注意深く観察しました。たとえば人がよく通る道は固くしまり、わらじのクズや馬糞が落ちています。木株の切り口や草刈りの跡が新しければ最近、人が来たしるしです。鳥や獣がひどく警戒するようなら人の往来が多いとわかるのです。

敵が**罠をしかけそう**な場所は、土を掘り起こした跡が残り、柔らかい土が表面に出ている。夜間に歩いている道が人の往来する道かどうかわからない時は、土をなめてみる。尿などが沁みて塩気がするようなら人や馬がよく通る道である……といったことに注意していました。

The Big Dipper revolves around Polaris once a day. This means that the constellation revolves 15 degrees an hour and 30 degrees every two hours. As the stars turn in such large degrees, ninja could know the rough time of every season. In addition, knowing the locations of the 28 constellations (the 28 *shuku* which are the 28 mansions in Chinese astronomy) enabled ninja to get directions more easily.

Q What is the ninja power of observation?

Having the power of observation was important as it enabled ninja to succeed in their tasks in unknown places. Ninja were very cautious about various locations. Some examples included busy streets, places where the soil could become solid and usually places where there were bits of straw sandals and horse droppings. If there were broken stumps or the traces of movement are new, this indicated that people had recently been there. Also, if birds and wild animals were very cautious, the area could be heavily used by people.

Moreover, in places where enemies were **likely to have set a trap**, there were usually traces of soil being dug up and uncovered soft soil on the surface of the ground. If ninja were not sure at night whether streets were used frequently by people, they tried licking the ground on the street. If the street was salty this is because it was soaked with urine and the like, which indicated that people and horses were coming and going there regularly.

Q 敵陣に潜入するタイミングはどうやって決めていましたか？

常に「虚」を突きました。相手が油断したり、疲れ果てていたり、極度に興奮していたりすると「実」を見失い、警戒に隙が生まれます。民家などの場合も、農作業で忙しい日が続いた後や冠婚葬祭を終えた直後などがそうでした。大雨や大雪などの天候も計算に入れました。また「陽動」として、火事や喧嘩などの騒ぎを起こして、進入路とは別の方向に注意を向かせる作戦もよく用いられました。

Q 忍者が使った暗号文はどんなものですか？

諜報こそ忍者の使命なので、自分が得た情報を秘密に伝える工夫をしました。まず入手した情報を記憶するのに、体の部位ごとに順番をつけ、1の情報は頭、2の情報は額、3の情報は目という風に「引き出し」を設けました。

あるいは、よく知る町の家並みの順に当てはめて覚える、身近なものに例える、大げさな話を作って忘れないようにするなどの方法を用いました。それらを記録したり、伝えるには普通の人に読まれないように古代の日本語といわれる「神代文字」や、「いろは」の50音をあらかじめ決めたコードで「偏と旁」に分けて書く「忍び

Q How did ninja decide when to infiltrate their enemy's camp?

Ninja always **seized an opportunity**. When opponents were careless, exhausted, and extremely agitated, they **lost sight of the reality** and became less vigilant. In private houses, this also happened frequently after people had had a busy day of working in the fields or soon after they had finished **ceremonial duties**. Ninja also considered weather conditions such as torrential rain and heavy snowfall. They often used **distraction tactics**. For instance, they would start a commotion such as a fire or a dispute as feint activities and this would make their enemies pay attention to a different direction than that of the imminent attack.

Q What secret words did ninja use as a cipher?

As espionage activities are indeed one of the ninja's main missions, ninja figured out a good way to transmit their obtained information secretly. First of all, in order to **learn the obtained information by heart**, they assigned a number to each of their body parts. For example, they associated information 1 with head, 2 with forehead, and 3 with eyes, and so on.

They also memorized information by using methods of applying the information to a row of houses in a well-known city, comparing information with familiar things, and making up exaggerated stories so as not to forget the information. In order to record or transmit information without it being read by ordinary people, they used *Jindai moji* and *shinobi moji* (stealth letters).

Special Techniques 🏹 59

文字」などを用いました。

神代文字

Q 情報伝達に「のろし」を使いましたか？

　敵の侵入など**危急の事態を味方に知らせる**場合、味方との距離が離れていれば、高い場所で「のろし」を上げてリレー方式で伝えました。煙は、地面に掘った穴に草やワラ、松葉などを入れて燃やし、太い竹の筒を煙突に使いました。燃やす材料や筒に蓋をする操作を変えることで色々な情報を送れました。

Jindai moji are said to be ancient Japanese letters and *shinobi moji* were written by dividing the fifty letters of *iroha* (traditional Japanese syllabary) into a left-hand and a right-hand radical with the code decided in advance.

忍び文字

つくり ＼ へん	木	火	土	金	水	人	身
色	い	ろ	は	に	ほ	へ	と
青	ち	り	ぬ	る	を	わ	か
黄	よ	た	れ	そ	つ	ね	な
赤	ら	む	う	ゐ	の	お	く
白	や	ま	け	ふ	こ	え	て
黒	あ	さ	き	ゆ	め	み	し
紫	え	ひ	も	せ	す	ん	

7つのへん、木・火・土・金・水・人・身に7つのつくり、色・青・黄・赤・白・黒・紫を組み合わせた文字を使っていたといわれている。これは敵にその内容が解読されないように工夫したものである

Q Did ninja use *noroshi* to transmit information?

To inform their comrades of critical situations such as the enemy's infiltration, when ninja were far away from the comrades they conveyed information by using a relay system that involved taking *noroshi* (a beacon) to high locations. To make *noroshi*, ninja put grass, straw, pine needles and the like into holes dug in the ground, burned the material, and used a big bamboo tube as the chimney. The burning of a variety of materials and the use of various procedures to cover the tube enabled ninja to send a range of information.

漢字で「狼煙」と書くのは、古代中国で狼の糞を入れて燃やすと、黒々とした見やすい煙になったことに由来します。味方が近くなら箱の中で燃やすタイプの「のろし」装置がありました。近距離なら旗や笛、ほら貝などを使いました。

Q **敵と味方を見分ける方法はどんなものですか？**

多数の人が参加する作戦では**味方の中に敵が潜入する**危険が高まります。そこで、**袖や笠に**目印の布を付けたり、「山」と言ったら「川」と答えるなどの「合言葉」や、耳や鼻をつまむなどの「合動作」を決めていました。

また、図柄を半分に割った「割り手形」で確認しました。会議の席などでも、ある言葉が発せられたらすぐに立ち上がるなどの「**決まりごと**」もありました。一緒に立たないものはその「決まりごと」を知らない敵とみなされました。

Noroshi means smoke of wolves in kanji. This is derived from the fact that in ancient China, when people burned feces of wolves by putting it as a fuel into a tube, a deep black smoke, which was easy to distinguish from other types, billowed out. Near the comrades, ninja used a box-shaped device in which to burn *noroshi*. Other signaling objects such as flags, flutes and trumpet shells were also useful.

Q How did ninja distinguish between their enemies and comrades?

There was an increased risk of **enemy infiltration among companions** when implementing strategies in which many people participated. Therefore, they put marked cloth on their **sleeves or sedge hats**. They also decided on passwords and secret actions such as holding their ears or nose. Various passwords were used. For example, if one ninja said "mountain," the other one would answer "river."

They also confirmed identification by *waritegata* (a divided board) whose pattern was cut in half. At a meeting, they performed the **usual secret actions** among their companions. For instance, as soon as one said a certain word, the others would stand up. Those who did not stand up immediately were regarded as enemies because they did not know the action required.

Q 何も書いてないように見せるワザもありますか？

　紙に薄い酸などで文字を書いて乾かすと、一見、何も書いてない紙に見えますが、**裏から熱であぶると**変色して文字が浮かびます。今でも、子どもがミカンの汁で字や絵を描く「あぶりだし」という遊びがあります。ミョウバン水でもできます。

　忍術の本には刻んだ大豆の汁か酒で書き、煤を振りかけて読む方法や、逆に、書いた証拠を残さないために、イカのスミで書き、乾燥した後に振り払えば落とせる方法が書かれています。

Q 忍者は「変装」の名人ですか？

　忍術書によると、「まず長い羽織などを着る。眉を描く、歯に金属をかぶせる、髪の生え際を剃って額を広げる、髪を乱すなどをするだけで印象がかなり変わる。他にも、墨や朱、黄土など塗って顔色を変える、付け髭、障害者の真似をするなどがあるが、あくまで不自然にならないようにすること。病人を装うなら、絶食し、風呂に入らず爪も伸ばすようなことまでしなけ

64 ✚ 特技

Q Did ninja have a technique for making invisible ink messages?

When you write letters with liquid like dilute acid on a piece of paper and dry them, at first sight it looks like the paper has no message on it. However, when **the back of the paper is heated**, the color of the letters changes and the invisible text becomes visible. Nowadays, there is also a game called *aburidashi* in which children write letters or draw pictures with orange juice or alum water, which does the same thing.

There is a *ninjutsu* book that explains a variety of techniques. For example, it describes various ways to write and then read invisible messages. For instance, if you can write letters with juice made from chopped soybeans or alcohol and sprinkle soot over the paper, the letters will become visible. Conversely, there is a way to make the letters invisible in order not to leave any written evidence: write the messages using squid ink and sweep them away after they have dried, and then the written messages will be erased.

Q Were ninja experts of disguise?

Yes indeed. One of the *ninjutsu* books explains: "Firstly, you should wear a long *haori* (Japanese half-coat), then pencil your eyebrows, cover your teeth with metal, widen your forehead by shaving your hairline and dishevel your hair. Using only these techniques enables you to change your appearance considerably. You can also use other techniques, such as changing the appearance of your face by putting on makeup

ればならない」と書かれています。

Q **忍者は、別の職業人に見せかけることも上手だったようですね？**

忍者は、人目につかぬようにして工作する「陰術」だけでなく、正体を隠して別人になって工作する「陽術」も使いました。

他の身分や職業に**変身する**のですが、各地を移動しても怪しまれないことが大事で、代表的なものが、虚無僧（普化宗の僧侶で深い笠をかぶり尺八を吹いて托鉢した）、出家、山伏、商人、大道芸人、役者などでした。

これも尺八や**経を読む**訓練が必要でした。七つ（7は、たくさんの意味）の顔を用意して出かけたので、この術を「七方出」と呼びます。しかし時代が移るにつれて、旅の僧や芸人などは真っ先に怪しい人物と見られるようになり、商人や**寺参りの旅行者**などに化けることが多くなりました。

66 ✦ 特技

with *sumi* (black ink), cinnabar, ocher, and the like, wearing a false beard or pretending to be a disabled person. Even so, bear in mind that you should behave naturally. If you pretend to be sick, you should fast, should not take a bath, and you should let your nails grow as well."

Q Ninja also seemed to be experts in disguising themselves as people with another occupation, didn't they?

Ninja used not only *yin jutsu*, but also *yō jutsu*. *Yin jutsu* is a technique that prevented ninja from being noticed and elaborating strategies. *Yō jutsu* is a technique that allowed ninja to modify their appearance and to pretend to be another person.

They **disguised themselves** as a person in a different position or having another occupation, even if traveling around various places because it was important for them not to arouse suspicion. Disguises were mainly in the form of *komusō* (the mendicant Zen priest of the *Fuke* sect known for wearing a sedge hood, playing the *shakuhachi*, and asking for religious alms), monks, mountain ascetics, merchants, street performers, actors and the like.

These occupations required training in playing the *shakuhachi* (the five-holed Japanese vertical bamboo flute) as well as in **chanting a sutra**. When going about their work, they prepared seven disguises, so this technique is called *shichihōde*. However, as time went by, traveling monks and performers were immediately viewed with suspicion. So ninja disguised themselves

Q なぜ女忍者は「くノー」というのですか？

「女」という漢字は、ひらがなの「く」とカタカナの「ノ」、漢字の「一」でできているからです。女性の忍者だけでなく、男性忍者が女装したり、ゲイ(陰間)を装うことも「くノー」忍法に含まれます。

男性が**主役になる**ことが**多い**政治や戦争の場面では、女性に対しては油断しがちです。そこで**敵陣に潜入したり**、要人に近づきやすくなります。その上、「くノー」も忍者としての**心得**と体術はしっかり身に着けているので立派に活躍しました。

Q 「忍者屋敷」とはどんなものですか？

忍者たちの住む屋敷には、いつ敵の襲撃があるかわかりません。そこで、家の周囲に縄を張っておき、触れると音が鳴るように竹で作った「鳴子」や落とし穴をしかけたり、塀には尖った金属や竹を置いて「**忍び返し**」にしました。

室内には、壁に仕掛けた**隠し扉**や、人が隠れるための**二重の壁**、天井裏の**隠し部屋**、落とし

68 **十** 特技

more frequently as merchants or as **travelers visiting a temple**.

Q Why were female ninja called *kunoichi*?

The reason why female ninja were called *kunoichi* is that *onna* written in Kanji consists of *ku* in hiragana, *no* in katakana and *ichi* in kanji. The term *kunoichi* covers not only female ninja, but also male ninja who disguised themselves as gay (*kagema*).

In political affairs and wars in earlier times men **often played the leading role**, so men tended to relax their guard around women. Thus it was easier for female ninja to **infiltrate the enemy's camp** and to get close to a very important person than it was for male ninja. In addition, *kunoichi* played an important role as ninja because they too possessed the **profound knowledge** of ninja and mastered *taijutsu* (unarmed combat).

Q Please explain the ninja house.

Ninja could not predict when their enemies might attack the ninja house. For that reason, they set a trap (pit) and *naruko* (clappers) made of bamboo around the house. *Naruko* made a rattling noise when someone touched the ropes which were stretched around and about the house. They also placed sharp-pointed metal and bamboo as **spikes** (a protective device) on the top of the fence.

In addition, they installed **hidden doors** behind the walls, **double walls** to hide themselves, **hidden rooms**

戸などを設けたりしました。また、家の裏の藪に逃げ込める地下道なども掘っていました。

忍者屋敷

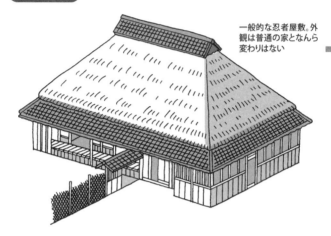

一般的な忍者屋敷。外観は普通の家となんら変わりはない

Q 忍者が使った「心理作戦」を教えてください

忍術には「陰」と「陽」があります。「陰」は**敵の眼を避けて侵入する**やり方。「陽」は、**普通の人になりきって**敵の中に入り込むやり方で、この方が多かったのです。

70 ✥ 特技

above the ceiling, and **trapdoors**. Furthermore, they made underground passageways in case they needed to escape into the bushes behind the house.

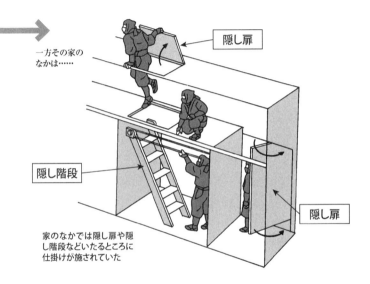

家の中のさまざまなカラクリ

一方その家のなかは……

隠し扉

隠し階段

隠し扉

家のなかでは隠し扉や隠し階段などいたるところに仕掛けが施されていた

Q Please tell me about the mind control technique used by ninja.

Ninjutsu has *yin* (negative) and *yō* (yang, positive) elements. *Yin jutsu* is a way of invading hostile territory by **diverting the attention of the enemy**. *Yō jutsu* is a way of infiltrating the enemy by **pretending to be an ordinary person**. This latter technique was used more often than *yin jutsu*.

深く信頼されて、相手が本心を話すように仕向けるには、高度な「**心理作戦**」が必要でした。「五車の術」というのは、人間が持つ5種の感情「喜・怒・哀・楽・恐怖」につけ込むものでした。

また「五欲の術」というのは、「食欲・性欲・名誉欲・財産欲・風流欲」という人間の欲望につけ込む術も駆使しました。「風流欲」というのは、芸事や骨董の収集など何らかの「趣味」に夢中になってしまう心理から生まれるものです。

Q **忍者は暗いところでもよく見えたのですか？**

夜間や暗い室内で行動することが多かった忍者は、暗闇でも視力を維持する訓練ができていました。ある忍術書には、暗闇での仕事に出かける際には「35日も前から、暗い所に籠って、目を慣らす」という方法が書かれています。**視覚**だけでなく、**嗅覚**、**味覚**、**聴覚**、**触覚**も敏感になるように日頃から鍛える工夫をしていたのです。

Q **忍者の他のトレーニング方法を教えてください**

忍者は常に**身体能力**を鍛えていました。速く、長く走っても疲れない走り方や、動作を俊敏に

In order to tempt enemies to trust ninja and to tell the truth, sophisticated **mind control** techniques were required. For example, the *gosha no jutsu* is the technique of taking advantage of a human's five emotions: *Ki* (Delight), *Do* (Anger), *Ai* (Sadness), *Raku* (Fun) and *Kyōfu* (Fear) which all people possess.

Ninja also had perfect command of *goyoku no jutsu*. This involved the technique of controlling a human's five desires: appetite, libido, eagerness for fame, greed for money, and eagerness having a passion for hobbies (*furyūyoku*). *Furyūyoku* results from the human feeling of having an obsession with a pastime such as watching performing arts and collecting antiques.

Q Were ninja able to see well in dark places?

As ninja spent a lot of working at night and in dark rooms, they usually had the chance to practice seeing in the dark. According to one of the *ninjutsu* books, ninja stayed in a dark place from 35 days prior to working in the dark. They usually strived to make opportunities for training on a day-to-day basis in order to become sensitive in not only the **sense of sight**, but also the **sense of smell**, the **sense of taste**, the **sense of hearing**, and the **sense of touch**.

Q Please tell me about another type of training undertaken by ninja.

Ninja always strived to improve their **physical abilities**. It was important for ninja to know how to run

する体の動かし方、長く呼吸を止める方法、敵との格闘術などはとても重要でした。

　そのためのトレーニングの一つに跳躍力を高める方法がありました。これは庭に**麻のタネを撒き**、その成長に合わせて徐々に高く跳べるようになるやり方です。麻は成長が速く、**人間の背丈**ぐらいに伸びます。徐々にその高さに慣れることで跳べるようになるのです。

　今でも忍者イベントなどに行くと、高さの違う縄やヒマワリなどを並べて跳躍力を試すコーナーがあります。

energetically even if they had to run long distances fast, how to move agilely, how to hold a long breathing which combat techniques to use against enemies, and the like.

They could master such techniques by improving their jumping power through training. To be more precise, first ninja **sowed hemp seeds** in the garden. Then, as the hemp grew taller, they jumped to the height of the plant and in this way were able to jump higher step by step. Hemp grows fast and as high as the **height of a person**. Therefore, they could learn to jump very high by getting used to jumping to the height of the plant little by little.

Nowadays, at ninja events, you can find a corner where objects of different height of such as ropes and sunflowers are placed and you can test your jumping power.

PART 3

道具
Tools

ニンジャの武器やコスチューム
Ninja Weapons and Costume

Q 手裏剣は本当に有効な武器ですか？

忍者の武器の代表格といえば手裏剣ですね。棒状のものから十字型、6ないし8方向に刃の付いた風車型などたくさんの種類があります。懐中に入れられる**携帯性**と**命中精度**と**殺傷力**とのバランスを考えた大きさで、近距離で使い、敵の攻撃をとめるには有効でした。刃先に毒薬を塗った使い方もあったようですが、首や胸などの急所に深く刺さらない限り即死させるのは難しかったはずです。

また火薬を巻き付けて投げる「手榴弾」のようなものも残されています。その投げ方も刃先を回転させるか否かで違いがあります。風車型手裏剣を掌にたくさん持ち、連続して投げるのは、1962年からのTV番組『隠密剣士』で演出されたもので、実際にはありません。手裏剣の命中率と威力については2005年に歴史雑誌が実験を行い、3mの距離で約5割の命中、二百数十ページの分厚い本を打ち抜くことができたとの結果もあります。

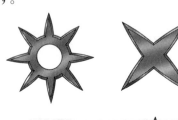

左上：八方手裏剣
右上：十字手裏剣
左下：六方手裏剣
右下：十方手裏剣

さまざまな手裏剣

Q Is a *shuriken* really an effective weapon?

A *shuriken* (a throwing star) is regarded as a **typical weapon of ninja**. It comes in a variety of shapes, ranging from stick-like to crisscrossed to windmill (flat) and has blades in six to eight directions. The size took into account the need for **portability** as it was placed next to the chest, as well as the need for **accuracy** and **killing power**. So it was an effective weapon in a fight at close range to stop the enemy's attack. It seems that some ninja applied poison to its cutting edge, but it would have been difficult to kill an enemy instantly unless it was stabbed deeply into the vital point of the neck or chest.

It was also used as a kind of hand grenade, where ninjas put gunpowder around a *shuriken* and threw it. There were two ways of throwing *shuriken* (by rotating the blade edges or not). In a Japanese TV program "The Samurai" (1962–1965), ninja held a lot of *shuriken* in their hands and threw them successively, but this differs from the historical fact. In 2005, a history magazine carried out an experiment in which they were able to hit and punch holes in thick books of over 200 pages from three meters away with an accuracy rate of around 50%.

八方手裏剣　　　十字手裏剣　　　流れ卍手裏剣

Tools 79

Q 「クナイ」というのは手裏剣の一種ですか？

[苦無(くない)]

三角形の**くさび型をした両刃の刃物**で、柄の元に輪のつくことが多い「クナイ(苦無)」は、壁や地面に穴を開けたりするのに便利な道具です。これを石垣や壁の隙間に差し込んで**足がかり**にもしました。武器として使う時は、輪に紐を通して振り回して使いました。丈夫な素材で作られているので、手裏剣のように使い捨てにはしませんでした。

Q 忍者の持つ刀と普通の刀の違いは？

忍者が活躍した時代、刀は切りやすいように**少し反っていました**。しかし忍者刀または「忍刀(しのびとう)」は長さが短めで刃はまっすぐで、これは携行しやすく、すばやく傷つける突きに向いています。その**鞘の先**には金属の尖ったキャップ（"こじり"という）が付いており、鞘のままでも武器にできました。他にも、その**鍔**が四角く大きいことや、下げ緒の紐が長いなどの特徴があります。これは塀などを越える時に紐をくわえ、壁に立てかけた刀の鍔に足をかけるのに便利です。

忍者は武士のように刀を腰帯に差すのではなく、刀を右肩から左腰にかけて背負うスタイルだと思われています。しかしこれでは抜ききれ

80 🏵 道具

Q Is a *kunai* a kind of *shuriken*?

A *kunai* (a ninja throwing knife) is a triangular, **wedge-shaped blade**, and it was a convenient tool when ninja needed to drill holes in the wall or the ground. Ninja also used it as a **foothold** by inserting it into a gap in stone fences or walls. When using it as a weapon, they put a string through a ring on the handle and swung it around. Unlike *shuriken*, a *kunai* was not disposable as it was made of more durable materials.

Q What are the differences between ninja swords and normal swords?

In the period when ninja were active, normal swords were **slightly arched** to make it easier to cut an enemy. In contrast, *ninjatō* or *shinobitō* (ninja swords) were shorter with a straight blade to increase portability. They were suitable for quickly stabbing enemies. A cap called a *kojiri* was attached to the **tip of the sheath**, so the sheath itself could also be employed as a weapon. Other distinctive features of *ninjatō* include their large, square **sword guards** and long *sageo* (a cord for attaching a sword scabbard tightly to the *obi*). These features made them handy when ninja had to put a rope in their month when crossing a fence or when they needed to put their feet on the sword guard to get up a wall.

You might think that ninja carried their sword from the right shoulder to the left hip, unlike a samurai who wore a sword in the waistband. However, it is

ないので、左肩から右腰に背負い、左手で支えながら右手で抜いたと思われます。しかし、実際にこのような刀も抜き方も伝わっていません。多くは明治以降の作りもので、実際には**頑丈な脇差し**程度のものを持ち、行動の邪魔になる時に背中に回したのではないかという説が有力です。

Q **弓などは使わなかったのですか？**

　大きな戦闘になる場合は、当然それらの武具も使いました。目立たず潜入して使うなら、「半弓（はんきゅう）」が便利でした。通常の大弓は2.2m、半弓といっても1.9m、これでも大きいので、実際に使われたのは1m前後の「短弓（たんきゅう）」だったと思われます。小型の弦ははずして別に携帯し、矢も短めのものを3本程度用意しました。殺傷力は強くないですが、**矢に毒を塗ったりして使った可能性はあります**。小説では、「**おりたたみ式の弓**」というのも登場しますが、どんな仕組みだったかは分かりません。

Q **「鍵縄（かぎなわ）」、「鎖鎌（くさりがま）」の使い方は？**

　縄や鎖の先に、金属製の碇（いかり）のようなものを付けたのが「鍵縄（かぎなわ）」で、これを投げ、木の枝や瓦の隙間などにひっかけてよじ登るのに使いました。また、先端に鎌を付けた「鎖鎌（くさりがま）」は、鎖のもう一端に重りの金属球（分銅（ふんどう））がついています。こ

82　道具

quite difficult to unsheathe a sword carried in this way, so they might have drawn it with the right hand with the support of the left hand. However, neither original *ninjatō* nor the unsheathing method has been handed down to the present day. Most of the existing *ninjatō* were invented in the Meiji period or later, and it is a popular theory that ninja had just a **sturdy, short sword** and put it on their back only when it got in the way of the action.

Q Did ninja use a bow?

Of course, they used such a weapon in large battles. A *hankyū* (a small bow) was a handy weapon when trying to infiltrate an enemy position inconspicuously. Normal large bows were 2.2 meters in length, and *hankyū* were 1.9 meters. So it is likely that ninja would actually have used a *tankyū* (a short bow) that was around 1 meter in length. They took off the bowstring and carried it separately, and took three or so short arrows with them. The killing power of these bows was not strong, but ninja might have **dipped the arrows into poison**. Some novels mention a **folding arrow**, but its details are unknown.

Q How did ninja use *kaginawa* and *kusarigama*?

A *kaginawa* is a rope or chain with a metal **grappling hook** in the shape of anchor attached to one end. Ninja slung it over a tree branch or into a gap between bricks to clamber up a wall. A *kusarigama* (a chain and sickle) is a weapon with a metal ball called a *fundō*

の重りの方を投げて直接攻撃するか、鎖で相手の刀や槍や体に巻き付けて使えなくしておき、**手に握った鎌**で相手を攻撃する武器です。

　鎖と鎌、分銅を分解して持ち運ぶことができるようにしたものや、両端が分銅になっているものなど多くの種類があります。

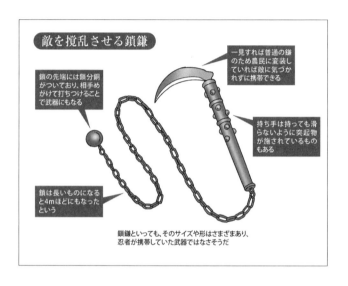

敵を撹乱させる鎖鎌

一見すれば普通の鎌のため農民に変装していれば敵に気づかれずに携帯できる

鎖の先端には鎖分銅がついており、相手めがけて打ちつけることで武器にもなる

持ち手は持っても滑らないように突起物が施されているものもある

鎖は長いものになると4mほどにもなったという

鎖鎌といっても、そのサイズや形はさまざまあり、忍者が携帯していた武器ではなさそうだ

Q　縄を伝ってよじ登るのは体が揺れてしまいませんか？

　縄よりも真っ直ぐな棒や竿の方が登りやすいです。長い竿の代わりに「一節竹管(ひとふしちっかん)」を使いました。**節を抜いた**ひと節（30cm前後）の竹を必要量用意し、間に**穴あき銭**を挟みながら次々と縄を通します。ふだんは畳んで携行し、使う時には縄の端を引っ張れば、竹が繋がって長い竿になります。穴あき銭は竹管と竹管のアジャス

84 🜛 道具

(weight) on one tip of the chain. Ninja threw this weight to attack an enemy directly, or put the chain around an enemy's sword or body to tie them up and then attacked the enemy by using **the sickle in their hand**.

There are many types of *kusarigama*, including ones that can be decomposed into a chain, sickle and weight, or ones with a weight on both ends.

Q Didn't their body sway when ninja climbed up a rope?

It is easier to climb up a straight bar or pole rather than a rope. So ninja used a *hitofushi chikkan* (a bamboo tube with one node) instead of a long pole. To make this device, they first prepared the necessary quantity of bamboo stems (about 30 cm in length). with their **nodes removed**. Then, they laid out the bamboo tubes end to end and put a **perforated coin**

Tools 85

ターになり、竹管の端を保護し、**登る足がかり**になりました。この綱の先に鉄の「鉤」をつけたものを「管鉤(くだかぎ)」と言いました。

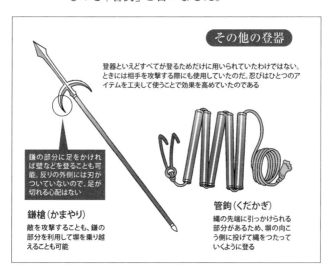

その他の登器

登器といえどすべてが登るためだけに用いられていたわけではない。ときには相手を攻撃する際にも使用していたのだ。忍びはひとつのアイテムを工夫して使うことで効果を高めていたのである

鎌槍（かまやり）
敵を攻撃することも、鎌の部分を利用して塀を乗り越えることも可能

鎌の部分に足をかければ壁などを登ることも可能。反りの外側には刃がついていないので、足が切れる心配はない

管鉤（くだかぎ）
縄の先端に引っかけられる部分があるため、塀の向こう側に投げて縄をつたっていくように登る

Q 「撒き菱」はどんな時に使うもの？

敵の追撃を遅らせたり諦めさせるために、廊下や道路に撒いて足に刺さるようにした武器です。もともとは、水草の一種で硬いトゲのある「菱の実(ひし)」を乾燥させてつかったことからこの名前がつきました。どのように蒔いても尖ったトゲの部分が上に向くようになっており、色々な形があります。また材質も植物の実や木、鉄、竹で作ったものなどがあります。

作り方は、材料の両端を尖らせた短い針にし、これを3本かみ合わせます。これらは竹の筒などにいれて持ち運びしましたが、かなりたくさ

between each of the tubes and passed a rope through the tubes and coins. They usually folded up and carried these bamboo tubes, and they just had to pull the ends of the rope to connect all the tubes together to make a long pole. The perforated coins could be used to adjust the bamboo tubes. They also protected the edges of the tubes and offered **footholds for climbing**. When an iron hook was attached to then end of a rope, it was called *kudakagi* (a tube with an iron hook).

Q When did ninja use a *makibishi*?

A *makibishi* (a Japanese caltrop) is a weapon that ninja placed in corridors or streets so that it would stick into enemies' feet and slow down or interrupt their chase. It was named after *hishi no mi* (a water chestnut) because it was originally made by drying a water chestnut, a kind of water plant with spiky thorns. They have a variety of forms, and their sharp thorny part always faces upward no matter how they are placed. They are usually made of tree nuts, wood, iron or bamboo.

The *makibishi* is made by sharpening both ends of the material into a short needle-like shape, and three of them are meshed together. *Makibishi* were carried

Tools 87

んの量が必要なので、集団で行動する時に使ったと思われます。また、追われてから撒くのでなく、あらかじめ想定される経路に撒いておき、自分たちは踏まないように「**すり足**」で抜けて通りました。同じような武器は中国や西洋にも見られ、また現代でも自動車のタイヤをパンクさせるのに使うこともありますね。

さまざまな変わり武器

角手

角手は忍者が持っていた武器のなかでも比較的小さいサイズだ

撒き菱

一個5グラム程度の軽さだったといわれる。形、太さ、大きさにバリエーションがみられる

鉄拳

先端が尖っているタイプ。ひとつの重さは200グラム程度なので携帯しやすい

鉄拳

敵に向ける側が刃になっているため、敵に深い傷を負わせることもできる

Q 手や指につける金属の「爪」は何ですか？

熊手のようにたくさんの刃がついたものを**手の甲**に装着するのを「手甲鉤」と言います。これは相手の刀の刃を受け止めたり、相手の手や顔を傷つけるのに使います。手早く穴を掘るのにも便利な道具です。石垣を登る際にも使いましたが、この時は刃が1本のものの方が実用的でした。

in a bamboo tube or the like. Ninja seemingly used them when they were acting in a group because they needed a lot of *makibishi* to make them effective. Ninja placed *makibishi* on the path along which their enemies were expected to travel instead of throwing them down when they were being chased, and walked in a **sliding manner** so that they would not step on them. There were similar weapons in traditional China and the West, and similar devices are still used today to puncture automobile tires.

Q What is the metal "claw" ninja wore on their hands and fingers for?

A *tekoukagi* (a hand claw) is a weapon with many blades like a rake that is attached to the **back of the hand**. It was used to block the blade of an enemy's sword or to hurt the hand or face of an enemy. It was also handy for digging a hole quickly. *Tekoukagi* were also used to climb up stone walls, but for this purpose, ones with only one blade were practical to use.

Tools 89

また、**メリケンサックのように**尖った鋲がついた指輪のようなものは、「角指」あるいは「万力」と呼ばれる武器です。メリケンサックと違うのは尖った鋲を手の内側に向けて装着すること。これは相手の顔をひっかいたり、手首や足首を握って食い込ませるためです。

Q 相手の攻撃をかわす「目つぶし」はどんな道具ですか？

映画などでは煙幕弾のようなものを使っていますが、実際に使われたのは相手の**涙腺を刺激する「目つぶし」**で、材料は鉄粉や塩、唐辛子粉など色々。胡椒はありません。

これを、小さく穴をあけて中身を抜いた卵の殻につめ、和紙で穴をふさいで作りました。相手の顔の傍に投げつけ、ひるんだ隙に身を隠したのです。

Q 水上を歩ける「浮橋」とはどんなもの？

幅の狭い堀などを渡るのに、いちいち「水蜘蛛」などを着けていたら手間取ります。とくに複数の忍者が渡るなら橋のようなものを架けて置く方が合理的です。そこで生まれた「浮橋」は、幅40cm弱で平行に張った10m程度の鎖の間に

They also used a ring-like weapon with sharp studs **like a brass knuckle**, which was called a *kakushi* (an iron ring with spikes) or a *manriki* (a vice). However, unlike a brass knuckle, this weapon was attached to the hand so that the sharp studs faced outward on the inside of the hand so that ninja could scratch the enemy's face or stab the studs into the enemy's wrist or ankle when they grabbed that part of their enemy's body.

Q What kind of methods did ninja use to dodge the attacks of their enemies?

In some movies, ninja use a smoke bomb, but what they actually used was a **potion to stimulate the enemy's lacrimal gland** that was made from various ingredients such as iron powder, salt or red pepper powder (black pepper was not used).

This blinding potion was made by emptying an eggshell by making a small hole in it, filling the shell up with the ingredients and then sealing the hole with Japanese paper. Ninja threw this device into their enemy's face and hid themselves when he recoiled.

Q What is the *ukihashi* that ninja used to walk on the surface of water?

It takes too long to cross a narrow moat wearing *mizu-gumo* (platter-shaped footwear). It is more sensible to build a bridge, especially when more than one ninja is going to cross the moat. So ninja invented an *ukihashi* (a floating bridge), which is a bridge made from two

幅の狭い板を5cm間隔で取り付けます。そして左右の縄の両端には鉄製のくさび。これで**「縄はしご」のようなもの**ができました。これを堀のこちら岸と向こう岸に突き刺して「浮橋」の完成。

足首までは水につかりますが、素早く渡ることができます。最初の取り付けだけは、誰かが堀を泳がねばなりませんが、逃走用や集団移動用には向いています。

Q 「つぼきり」も忍者の必携道具だと聞きました

穴を開ける「錐」と違うのは、先端が2つに分かれていること。片方を板や壁に突き刺しておいて、もう一方の刃を**コンパスのように回すことで穴を開けることができます**。その穴から中の様子をのぞいたり、板戸に取り付けられた内

開器の利用法

坪錐（つぼきり）
回転させることで直径20センチほどの穴を開けることまで可能だ

壁に押し当て左右に回す

parallel chains that looks **somewhat like a rope ladder**. The chains were around 10 meters in length and were placed less than 40 cm apart. Narrow plates were fixed to these two chains at intervals of 5 cm and iron wedges were attached to the ends of the chains. Ninja stuck the iron wedges into both banks of the moat and thus made a floating bridge.

By using this device, they could cross a moat quickly though their feet would have got soaked. Also, someone had to swim in the moat to install the bridge, but it was suitable for escaping or for group movements.

Q I heard that *tsubokiri* was an essential ninja tool.

A *tsubokiri* (a round drill) is different from a gimlet in that its tip is divided into two blades. Ninja could make a hole by sticking one blade into the plate or wall and rotating the other blade, similar to **drawing a circle with a compass**. They could then peep inside

錏(しころ)
壁に当てて動かせば
簡単に木製の板や壁
などを切り抜ける

Tools 93

側のカンヌキなどをはずすのに便利。いざとなれば武器としても使えます。

　刃がのこぎりのようになっている「しころ」という道具も同様の目的で使います。

Q **床下や天井に潜んでいながら敵の話が聴こえたのですか?**

　節を抜いた竹筒や、鉄や木で**円錐状にした道具**を使ったと思われます。昔の補聴器と同じ原理です。床下などの場合は、「些音聞金」という薄い**金属製の共鳴板**を吊り下げて、音を増幅して聴いていたという記録があります。これは「小さな音も聴ける金属板」の意味です。

Q **生垣のように密生した植え込みを抜ける時はどうしましたか?**

　「桶抜き」といって、桶の底を抜いてそれを生垣の中に押し込み、できた空間を抜けるように工夫しました。これは持ち歩く忍具ではなく、手近なところにあったものを道具として使う例です。いくら便利でも、何でも持ち歩くわけにはいかないので、こういう臨機応変の工夫が求められたのです。

94　道具

a room through the hole and could also remove an inside bolt attached to a sliding door through the hole. *Tsubokiri* could also serve as a weapon in a combat.

A *shikoro* (a kind of a double-edged saw) is an instrument that is also used for a similar purpose.

Q Could ninja hear enemies talking while they were hiding beneath the floor or on the ceiling?

Ninja seemingly used a hollow bamboo tube or a **cone-shaped device** that was made out of iron or wood, based on the same principle as a hearing aid. Also, they reportedly suspended a **thin-metal sounding board** called a *saoto kikigane* to amplify sound for the purpose of eavesdropping. *Saoto kikigane* literally means a metal board that enables you to hear small sounds.

Q How did ninja go through dense vegetation like hedges?

They knocked out the bottom of a wooden tub (*okenuki*) and put it into the hedge and went through the space created. This would not have been an instrument they carried with them—they would have used something like it that was near at hand as a makeshift tool. They could not carry all the tools that they might need, so they had to be resourceful as the occasion demanded.

Q マッチやライターのようなものは持っていましたか？

火打ち石で発火させ、繊維質のものをほぐした「火口（ほくち）」に移して火種にするのが昔の着火法。忍者の場合は、この「火口」に硫黄などをしみこませた小さな竹串を使いました。これを「付竹（つけだけ）」と呼びます。桧や杉の小さな板で作ったものは「付木（つけぎ）」です。

Q 移動しながら使えた照明道具があったのですか？

昔の懐中電灯ですね。「ガンドウ」といって、木や鉄製の桶の中に鉄の輪を2重に組込み、外側の輪だけを桶側につけ、回転してもろうそくを立てた内側の輪だけは水平になるようにしたのが「ガンドウ」（龕灯）です。オモチャの「地球ゴマ」と同じジャイロの原理です。これなら消えずに進行方向だけを照らせます。

強盗（がんどう）が使ったので「強盗提灯（がんどうぢょうちん）」の名もあります。ただし江戸時代に工夫され、捕り手や普通の人にも使われていました。

Q Did ninja have something like a match or a lighter?

People used to **strike a flint** and then transferred the spark to *hokuchi* (tinder made out of loose fibers) and used it to start a fire. Ninja used small bamboo skewers impregnated with sulfur as tinder, called *tsukedake* (bamboo tinder). If the tinder was made from a small wooden plate of Japanese cypress or cedar, it was called *tsukegi* (touchwood).

Q Did ninja have a portable light source?

Yes, they had a tool corresponding to a modern flashlight. It was called a *gandō* (portable lighting apparatus). It is made up of a double iron ring placed in a wooden or iron tub, in which the outer ring of the two is attached to the inside of the tub and the inner ring that holds a candle remains horizontal. It is based on the **principle of the gyroscope**, like the Japanese science toy *chikyū gom*a ("Earth" spinning top). This design prevented the fire from dying out and allowed ninja to light up the direction in which they were traveling.

As it was also used by robbers (also called *gandō*), it was also called a *gandō chōchin*. However, it became popular among arresting officers and ordinary people in the Edo period.

Q 寒い時に"張り込み"する場合はどんな工夫をしていましたか？

今のように振るだけで発熱する使い捨てカイロが普及する前は、金属容器のベンジン油を燃やすものや、木炭やナスの茎、桐の灰などを燃やす懐炉がありました。忍者が使ったのは、布を固く巻いて蒸し焼き（炭化）したものを金属の筒にいれた「胴の火」というものです。これを懐に入れておけば半日ぐらいは温かかったようです。

Q 忍者の衣装について教えてください

忍者といえば、顔を頭巾で隠し、上下とも黒っぽい衣をつけ、黒足袋にわらじというイメージが浮かぶと思います。これは暗闇に紛れて活動する時のもので、日中ではかえって目立ちます。

戦闘が想定される場合は、下着に鎖で編んだ「鎖帷子」を付け、頭巾は一枚の布を頭から顔まで覆うようにして巻き付けます。衣の色は赤茶けた黒、茶褐色、紺色など地味なもの。下に履く股引は、膝まではゆったりしていて、脛から下は「脚絆」などで絞っていました。ポケットがたくさんあったり、裏表で色が異なるリバーシブルになっていました。武田流の忍術では、衣装をつける前に、脚にヒマシ油を塗り、夜露や虫刺されなどから守る方法があります。帯は縄のようにして使うこともできるものです。**柿渋を塗って防水処理した雨合羽**も便利なものでした。

98 　道具

Q What did ninja do when they went on a stakeout when it was cold?

Before the invention of the disposable pocket warmer that generates heat when you shake it, people burnt gasoline in a metal box or charcoal, eggplant stems, or paulownia ashes in a *kairo* (pocket heater). However, ninja used *dōnohi*, which consisted of a metal cylinder into which they placed cloth that was tightly rolled and then smothered (carbonized). It could remain warm for half a day in their inside pocket.

Q What did ninja wear?

You may associate ninja with dark figures who wear black clothes, black split-toe socks and straw sandals and hide their face with a hood. This clothing is for night activities in the dark; it would stand out a lot in the daytime.

When they expected to engage in a fight, they wore *kusari katabira* (chain mail) as an undergarment and wound a piece of cloth around their head and face to cover their face. The colors of their clothes were plain, like reddish black, brown or navy blue. The *momohiki* (drawers) they wore under their pants were loose from the waist to the knees, and below the shins they were gathered up by *kyahan* (gaiters with drawstrings). *Momohiki* had a lot of pockets or different colors on the front and back. In Takeda-ryū (Takeda School) *ninjutsu*, ninja applied castor oil to their legs before putting on clothes in order to protect their body from night dew or insect bites. The belt could also be used

忍び装束のイメージ

- 頭巾は一枚の布を顔全体に巻くように覆っていた
- 上着は動きやすさを重視して調整可能だったといわれる
- 口と鼻の大部分を隠し必要最低限の部分しか敵にさらさない
- 手甲は外傷から身を守るだけでなく寒さから身をしのぐためのものでもあった
- 忍者＝刀をつねに携帯するイメージだが、つねに日ごろ持ち歩いていたわけではない
- 草鞋の裏には滑り止めがついており、俊敏に動けるようになっていた
- 脛の部分は袴の上から脚絆という衣類を身に纏っていた。これは足に草木や砂利などが入り込まないように工夫されたもの

すべての忍者が上記のような忍び装束を着ていたわけでない。われわれが思い浮かべるのは作られた忍者イメージといっても良い

Q　忍者は笠や手ぬぐいも使いましたか？

ふだんは**目立たぬようにしたい**ので、笠をかぶって顔を隠すのが普通でした。1mより少し長い大き目の手ぬぐいも必需品で、頬かむりし

100　道具

as a rope. **A waterproof raincoat coated with persim-mon tannin** was also a useful garment.

Q Did ninja use a *kasa* or a *tenugui*?

Ninja usually wore a *kasa* (straw lampshade-like hat) to hide their face and **keep a low profile**. A fairly big *tenugui* (cotton towel) slightly longer than 1 meter

て顔を隠したり、汗を抑えるのに頭にまいたり、水をろ過して呑んだり、切れたわらじの緒代わりや傷の手当の包帯にも使い、石をくるんで振り回したり投石の武器としても使えました。

Q 敵の人数や武器の数え方、それらを記録する筆記具はどうしましたか？

あらかじめ決まった数の豆や小石を袋に入れ、数えるたびにそれを除きました。残った石の数で数えた数値がわかります。それを紙などに記録する際、普通の旅行者は「矢立」といって筆と墨を納めた**携帯文具**を使いましたが、それが無い場合、黒紫の柔らかい石を穂先のように削って、竹筒にはめて鉛筆代わりにしました。

Q 「五色米」というのはどういうものですか？

米を、赤、青、黄、黒、紫の5色に染めたもので、忍者どうしが道路脇などに目立たぬよう置く情報伝達の道具です。色と数の組合せで**100種類以上の暗号**に使えました。色がついているので、鳥などに食べられることもほとんどなかったとか。単純な暗号なら、枝や数個の石、草を結ぶ方法などでも十分でした。これは今でもボーイスカウトが教わる方法です。

was also a must. They used it to cover and hide their face, put it around their head to suppress sweating, filtered water with it before drinking, and used it as a substitute for a broken thong on *waraji* (straw sandals), as a bandage to treat a wound, or as a weapon to wrap around stones and swing or throw them.

Q What were the ninja counting systems for the number of enemies or weapons, and what writing tools did they use for recording such figures?

They put a **predetermined number** of beans or small stones in a bag and took one out each time they counted "1". The number of remaining beans or stones showed them the number they had counted. To record something on paper, like ordinary travelers they used a *yatate*, which is a **portable writing set** with a brush and ink. If this was not available, they carved a soft black-purple stone into the shape of the tip of a writing brush and put it into a bamboo tube. Then they used it as a pencil.

Q What is *goshokumai*?

Goshokumai is five-colored rice (red, blue, yellow, black and purple). Ninja used it as a method of communication—they placed it inconspicuously beside the road etc. Its color/number combination produced **more than 100 types of ciphers**. Birds rarely ate it because it was colored. By the way, they also used a simpler method of tying up some branches, or gathering together several stones or pieces of grass. Boy scouts still use these methods today.

Tools 103

Q 「火薬」はどうやって作っていましたか？

　　忍者は最先端の化学知識の持ち主でした。黒色火薬の主な原料は木炭粉と硫黄と硝石（硝酸カリウム）です。一番入手しにくい硝石は、草と動物の糞尿などを混ぜて土の中に５年くらい埋めて置き、その土ごと水に溶かします。

　　次にこの溶液に木灰を入れて煮詰め、ろ過し乾燥させると塩の一種である硝酸カリウムの結晶ができました。これらの配合比率を変えたり他のものを混ぜることで、黒煙がたくさん出るものから大きな爆発を起こすものまで色々な火薬が作れました。その製法はそれぞれの流派の秘伝でした。

Q 「火薬」の種類をもっと知りたいので教えてください

　　火薬を使う「火術」は、使い過ぎることは諫められました。それでも忍術書には200以上の作り方や使い方が書かれており、**化学的に納得できるもの**もあります。

　　硝石を増やすと火力が増す、馬糞を混ぜると火持ちがよい、硫黄を増やすと青く強い炎になる、樟脳を増やすと火が弱く燃える……等々。矢に推進ロケットを付けて数百ｍ先まで飛ばす

104 ✜ 道具

Q How did ninja make gunpowder?

Ninja had innovative knowledge of chemistry. The main ingredients of black gunpowder are charcoal powder, sulfur and saltpeter (potassium nitrate). Saltpeter was the least readily available ingredient. To make it, first, a mixture of grasses and animals dung was buried in the ground for about five years, and then the soil containing the decomposed mixture was dissolved in water.

Then, wood ash was added to the solvent and the solvent was boiled down, filtered and dried to obtain crystals of potassium nitrate, a kind of salt. By changing the blending ratio or mixing it with other ingredients, it was possible to make various types of gunpowder, ranging from one that produced huge plumes of black smoke to one that caused big explosions. The production method of each school was secret.

Q Please tell us more about the varieties of gunpowder.

Ninja were discouraged from overusing *kajutsu* (using fire with gunpowder). However, a book on *ninjutsu* shows how to make and use more than 200 kinds of gunpowder, and some of them are **chemically convincing**.

Some descriptions are as follows: increasing the proportion of saltpeter will add firepower, mixing horse dung will keep the fire burning longer, increasing the proportion of sulfur will make the flame blue

「大国火矢」については、飛ばしたい距離ごとの成分比率まで書かれています。

Q 薬や毒薬などはどんなものがありますか?

　伊賀・甲賀一帯の里山は**薬草**の産地でしたから、それらをどう使いこなすかの知恵は古くから蓄積されていました。やけどや切り傷、捻挫などの外傷に効く薬や、回虫や下痢、カゼに効く薬を常備していました。また敵に対しては、トリカブトの根や昆虫のハンミョウのように暗殺のための毒薬、いぶした煙で**幻覚を起こさせる**大麻、下痢・腹痛を起こすノウルシなどが使われました。薬と毒薬は**表裏一体なの**です。

Q 犬が忍者の大敵だったのは本当ですか?

　本当です。犬は不審者には吠えたてるし、追い払おうとすれば反撃し、仲間がすぐに集まる動物です。だから忍術書では犬対策を取り上げています。例えば、焼きおにぎりで手なずける。あるいは、オスにはメスというように、異性の犬を向けて気をそらせる。それでも駄目なら「犬殺し」を使います。これは焼きおにぎりの中に、「マチン(馬銭子。別名ホミカ)」というアルカロ

106 　道具

and stronger, increasing the proportion of camphor will make the fire weaker. The book also describes the ratio of ingredients needed to make a *daikokuhiya* (a big bow to shoot an arrow with a fiery propulsion rocket hundreds of meters) fly the desired flight distance.

Q What kinds of medicine and poison did ninja use?

The forests around the villages in Iga and Kōga produced **medicinal herbs**, so ninja were able to accumulate knowledge about how to use them. This meant that ninja always had medicine for injuries such as burns, cuts, and sprains as well as for diarrhea and colds. Also, they used poisons for assassination such as aconite roots and tiger beetles, cannabis whose fumigate smoke **causes hallucinations**, or euphorbia adenocholora that causes diarrhea or a stomachache. Medicines and poisons are **two sides of the same coin**.

Q Is it true that dogs were formidable enemies of ninja?

Yes. Dogs bark at strangers and fight back if you try to drive them away. Also, they tend to band together if something happens. So books on *ninjutsu* explain how to take care of dogs such as taming dogs with grilled rice balls or sending in dogs of the opposite sex to distract guard dogs. If these measures did not work, ninja used "dog killers," which were grilled rice balls mixed with the seeds of a poisonous herb containing

イドのストリキニーネを含む毒草の種子成分を入れたものです。強烈な全身麻痺を起こし呼吸困難になって死にます。江戸時代には殺鼠剤、殺虫剤にも広く使われました。

Q 武器ではないですが、「携行食」も必需品ですね？

　その通り。当時の人は１日２食でしたが、遠いところに出かけたり、**敵陣でじっと待機**しなければならない時には「携行食」が必要でした。一般の人は、炊いたご飯を水で洗ってから５日ほど干した「干飯」を使いました。熱湯で戻せば柔らかく食べられます。

　材料や作り方は実にさまざまで、戦国時代の武者たちが用いたのは、味噌やもち米、木の実などをまぜて団子にして乾かした「兵糧丸」です。また、「飢渇丸」といって、人参、山芋、はと麦、そば粉などを練った非常食もあったようです。

　携行食ではないですが、**籠城する場合に**備えて、城の壁には保存の効くスルメを塗りこんでおくことも当時の常識でした。

a kind of alkaloid (strychnine) called nux vomica. This causes intense general paralysis and dyspnea that leads to death. In the Edo period, the herb was also widely used as a rodenticide or an insecticide.

Q Ninja always brought field rations with them, didn't they?

Yes. In those days, people ate twice a day, but when they had to go on a long journey or watch and **wait at the enemy's camp**, they needed field rations. Ordinary people used *hoshiii* (dried boiled rice), which was made by washing cooked rice with water and then drying it for about five days. You can soften it with hot water before eating it.

There are a lot of variations in the ingredients and recipes. For example, in the Age of the Warring States ninja used *hyōrōgan* (military ration pills), a mixture of miso, glutinous rice and tree nuts etc. that was made into dumplings and dried. Also, they kneaded ginseng, yam, Job's tears and buckwheat etc. to make emergency provisions called *kikatsugan* (another kind of military ration pills).

By the way, it was common practice to put preserved dried squid into castle walls in **preparation for a siege**.

PART 4

思想
Thoughts

ニンジャたちの生き方を貫く哲学
Ninja Philosophy, Keeping the Faith

Q 「忍」という漢字には特別な意味がありますか？

　辞書的には「**世間の人の目を避けて隠れる**」とか、「**自分の感情を抑え、じっと我慢して耐える**」という意味になります。忍者の世界では、この「忍」が「心という字に、刃を乗せている」文字であると解釈して、緊張感を常に持ちながら、自分をいましめ、耐える状態が忍者の心得であると説きます。

　忍者の使命は、「世の中から隠れるようにして静かに暮らしていても、いざとなれば大きな仕事成し遂げる」ことです。この意志と緊張感を失って私欲に流される時、死を招くことになります。

Q 「**よい忍者**」になれる条件はありますか？

　江戸時代でも初期の頃に書かれた軍学書では、「忍びに使うのによい人は、1に知恵があること、2に記憶力のよい人、3に口の上手な人」と書き、そういう人は伊賀甲賀衆だとすすめています。これが60年ぐらい後の忍術書になると要件は「十か条」になり、「忠勇、義理」の心、柔和な性格、欲が少ないこと、妻子や家族も行いが正しいこと、諸国の事情をよく知り、詩や謡、舞なども上手で「間つなぎ」できること……などと、やたらと道徳的で、仕事も遊びも完璧な人物像を描いています。世の中が落ち着いて、忍者として生きるより奉公先で気に入られることが大事になってきた世相を映しているように思えます。

112 　思想

Q Does the kanji "忍" have a special meaning?

"忍" literally means "**to shun the public eye and hide**" or "**suppress one's feelings, and endure patiently**." In the ninja world, "忍" (*shinobu*) was interpreted as "刃" (blade) sticking onto "心" (heart), and ninja were urged to have a sense of tension, admonish themselves and be patient.

The ninja's mission was to accomplish a big job when it came to the crunch even if they usually hid from the world and lived quietly. If they lost this determination and sense of tension and instead pursued their own interest, this would lead to their death.

Q Are there any requirements for being a good ninja?

A book about military science written in the early Edo period says "an eligible person to be a *shinobi* is: (1) a person of wisdom, (2) a person of good memory, and (3) a smooth talker," and Iga or Kōga ninja are such persons. In a book on *ninjutsu* published a bit later, the requirements were summed up in 10 points: loyalty, bravery, gentle personality, a low level of desire for material things, their wives and children are doers of good, detailed knowledge of the circumstances of various regions, expertise in poems, *Noh*-chants and dances so that they can entertain others, etc. This describes a highly ethical person who is perfect at work and play. It seems to reflect the social conditions of a society that had calmed down and in which it had

Q 忍者が約束を誓う時の儀式はどんなもの？

　忍者は基本的にチームワークで行動するので互いに裏切らないことが重要でした。そこで「起請文」と言って**結束を誓う**文章「神文」を2部作成し、1部は神社に奉納し、もう1部は、焼いて灰にしたものを酒（お神酒）に入れて回し飲みしました。これを「一味神水」と言います。「一味」というのは仲間、チームのこと、「神水」というのは神文を灰にしたお神酒のことです。

Q **忍者の生活がストイック（禁欲的）というのは本当？**

　忍者の倫理感や忠誠心は時代とともに変化しました。初期には強盗まがいのことをしていましたが、戦国時代から傭兵となり、江戸期には各藩に雇用される身分になり、**藩主に忠誠を尽くす**ことが大事になりました。「その命は主君に捧げたものだから、私的なことで身を亡ぼすようなことがあってはならない。とくに、**酒**と**色**と**欲**に溺れることは堅く禁ずる。これらは本心を失わせる敵である」と書いた忍術書もあります。

114 🥢 思想

become more important to be liked by an employer than to live as a ninja.

Q What was the ritual that ninja followed when making an oath?

Ninja basically acted in a team so it was important not to betray each other. So they made a written vow called *shinmon* to **swear solidarity**, in duplicate; one copy was dedicated to a shrine and the other copy was burnt to ashes. They put the ashes into *omiki* (sacred sake) and passed round the cup to drink it in turn. This ritual is called *Ichimi-shinsui*. *Ichimi* means companions or team and *shinsui* means sacred sake with *shinmon* that is reduced to ashes.

Q Was the ninja's life really stoic?

The sense of ethics and the loyalty of ninja changed with the times. In the early days they were not much different from robbers, but in the Age of the Warring States they became mercenaries (soldiers). In the Edo period, ninja were employed by domains, and their principal mission was to **show loyalty to daimyo** (feudal lords). A book of *ninjutsu* even says, "Your life is dedicated to the lord, so you should not ruin yourself with a private matter. Especially, it is strictly prohibited to give yourself over to **drink**, a **woman's beauty**, or other **worldly indulgences**. These are the enemies that make you lose your mind."

Thoughts 115

Q 忍者の唱える呪文にはどんな意味がありますか?

2章の「特技」のQ&Aで「九字の印」を説明しましたが、これは9つの神様に自分を守ってもらう護身の呪いです。もう一つ、敵から身を隠して戦いに勝つ「隠形の印」があります。この印を結びながら**唱える呪文**が「オン・アニチ・マリシエイ・ソワカ」です。「マリシエイ」はインド伝来の軍神で女神の「摩利支天」のこと。印の中心となる動作は左手の拳を右手でくるむように握り、キリスト教の**十字切りを逆にしたような順序**で体の各部に当てます。陰陽道や修験道を研究した山伏の信仰や**密教**の影響があり、「摩利支天」は戦国武将たちからも信仰されました。

Q 忍術の元祖が「役小角」という説がありますね

山岳地帯を巡って厳しい修行をする「山伏」と忍者の行動はよく似ています。当時の考えでは、最新の科学と心理学を体を使って研究する人たちだったかもしれません。

そんな修験道行者の祖先と言われるのが「役小角」、別名「役行者」です。生没年(634年-701年)の記録も残る実在の人物ですが実像は不明です。**岩窟に住み、葛の衣を着て、松の葉を喰い、清泉を身に浴びるなどの修行を重ねた**結果、呪術で鬼神を使役して雑用をやらせたり、「孔雀明王」の呪文で毒や災難を取り除きまし

Q What meaning does a ninja's spell have?

Like *kuji no in*, a kind of hand gesture to ask the nine gods for protection (as we discussed in Chapter, 2), *ongyō no in* was another hand gesture that they used to hide themselves from enemies and win a battle. They made a hand gesture and **cast a spell**, "*Om Āditya Mārīcī Svāhā.*" Marici is a goddess of war from India. To make the hand gesture, they clasped their left fist with their right hand, and placed their hands on various parts of their body in **reverse order to make the sign of the cross**. Under the influence of *onmyōdō* (the way of *yin* and *yang*), *yamabushi shinkō* (belief in mountain priests who pursued mountaineering asceticism) and **Tantric Buddhism**, Marici was worshiped by samurai in the Warring States Period.

Q Some believe that Enno Ozuno was the pioneer of *ninjutsu*.

The behavior of *yamabushi* (mountain priests) who undergo harsh training in the mountains is quite similar to that of ninjas. Ninja may have been considered to be people experimenting with the latest scientific and psychological knowledge in the field.

The pioneer of such practitioners of mountaineering asceticism is Enno Ozuno, a.k.a. Enno Gyōja. His dates of birth and death are known (634–701) but we have no idea what he was like; **he lived in a grotto, wore clothes made from kudzu vine, ate pine nuts, and bathed in water from a pure fountain**. By virtue of such training, he could reportedly use magic to

Thoughts 117

た。讒訴によって伊豆島に配流されても、夜になると空を飛んで富士山で修行したと言われます。彼を祀る遺跡は全国にあります。

Q 忍術の本で、忍者は「正心」第一とあるのはどんな意味？

「正心」とは心を正しくコントロールすること。そのためには、「仁義・忠信」を**守る心が作られていなければなりません。仁義は人としての正しい行い**、忠信とは忠義と信実で、誠実で正直なことです。これができなければ、臨機応変の計略を遂行することができません。

その根本に「仁義・忠信」がなければ、私欲のために忍術を行って利益を得ようとすることになり、それは盗賊と同じである。また**非道の君主**を助けて悪いたくらみをおこなっても必ず露見する。……と書いている本があります。

Q 忍術と「禅」にはどんな関係がありますか？

13世紀（鎌倉時代）に中国から伝来した禅宗の教えは、長い時間をかけながら日本的な禅に変わり、徐々に広く知られるようになりました。

江戸期前半に書かれた忍術書は、**武士の心得**

make demons do various chores, or cast spells to get rid of poison or disasters. He was banished to Izu island based on a false charge, but legend says that he flew in the sky to Mt. Fuji and kept training himself at night. The old shrines that worship him are found nationwide.

Q A book on *ninjutsu* says ninja should keep *seishin*. What does it mean?

Seishin means to control your mind in a just manner. To this end, ninjas should **be ready to stand firm in** their *jingi* (humanity and justice) and *chūshin* (fidelity). *Jingi* is a **righteous action as a human being**, and *chūshin* means loyalty and honesty. If they cannot observe these principles, they cannot take tactical measures as the situation demands.

A book on *ninjutsu* says that ninjas should act on *jingi* and *chūshin*, or they will be nothing more than thieves as they intend to gain profit and benefit themselves by using *ninjutsu*. It also says that, if a ninja helps an **unconscionable master** to devise an evil scheme, it will always be discovered.

Q What is the relationship between *ninjutsu* and zen?

The teaching of zen (Buddhism), which was derived from China in the 13th century (during the Kamakura period), changed into a Japanese-style zen over a period of time and gradually became widely known.

A book of *ninjutsu* from the early Edo period

になっていた禅の思想を踏まえ、その価値観で**忍術の極意**を解説します。たとえば、平常心の大切さ、相手の警戒心を取り除くこと、奥義の本質は言語化できないこと（「不立文字」）などと書かれています。これらはそれまでの実用本位な「古い忍術」の価値観とは違っており、また中国の『孫子』が「間」と呼んだ中国忍者たちとも違うものです。

Q もっと身近な忍者の「心得」はないのですか？

　忍者と座禅では、なんとなく似合わないですね。もっと簡単な言葉で、**忍者の心得**を書いた書物もあります。そこには「忍者には危険が3つある。第1は**恐怖心**、第2は**敵を軽んずる心**、第3は**思案を過ごす（考えすぎる）こと**」とあります。これらによって「**優柔不断になり、好機を見逃し、禍を招いてしまう**」からです。筆者は、ポジティブに考えて行動してみれば、心配するほどのことはなく、勝利に繋がることもあると言いたいのです。

120 　思想

states that **the secrets of ninjutsu** were based on the thoughts and values of zen, which had then been the **precepts of samurai**, including the importance of a calm mind, removal of the opponent's caution, and the indescribable nature of secret lore (*furyū-monji*). These are different from the values of old practical *ninjutsu* and from those of Chinese ninjas, whom Sun Zi (an ancient writer who wrote *The Art of War*) in China called "*kan*."

Q Are there any mottos that might be more familiar to us?

Doesn't zen match the image of ninja? Well, there is another book that explains the **mottos of ninjas** in simpler way, saying, "Ninjas face three dangers—**fear**, **making light of the opponent**, and **thinking too much**," as these might "**make them indecisive**, **miss a chance or invite a disaster**." The author implies that things may be easier than expected, so acting positively may lead to victory.

伝説
Legends

ニンジャのエピソードやレジェンド
Ninja Episodes and Legends

Q 能の「観阿弥、世阿弥」親子は忍者だった？

　昔は「猿楽」などと呼ばれた能楽師たちは旅をしながら芸を見せました。それは忍者がよく化ける職業（「七方出」）であり、忍者が住む地域から発生しています。

　とくに1331年生まれで猿楽能の大家である観阿弥は、父が伊賀・服部一族の服部元成、母がゲリラ戦に強かった楠木正成の姉（または妹）ですから、**まさに忍者の家系**。

　そして観阿弥の息子が能を**大成した**世阿弥です。他にも、忍者や山師（鉱山開発者）を束ね、金山開発で巨万の富を蓄えながら殺された大久保長安も若い頃は能役者でした。大いに怪しいのです。

Q 鉱山開発の専門家「山師」たちも忍者ですか？

　豊臣秀吉が政権を握る頃から全国で金山や銀山の算出量が急増しました。その背後には前のQ&Aで紹介した大久保長安など、旧武田家お抱えだった鉱山開発のプロ集団「山師」の活躍があります。開発や精錬のノウハウは秘密でした。彼らは、全国の山々を伝って移動し、独自の生活スタイルと情報網を持っていたのです。

Q Were the father and son *Noh* players Kan'ami and Zeami ninja?

Noh was originally called *sarugaku*, and *Noh* players went on tour and performed *sarugaku*. One of the *shichihōde* (seven ninja disguises) was that of a *sarugaku* performer, and *sarugaku* plays originated from the areas in which ninja lived.

Kan'ami, who was born in 1331 and was a master performer of *sarugaku*, had a father Hattori Motonari who belonged to the Iga Hattori clan and a mother who was a sister of Kusunoki Masashige, a samurai who excelled in guerrilla warfare. So he seems to have been born into the **perfect family to become a ninja**.

Zeami was the son of Kan'ami, and brought *Noh* performance to the **pinnacle of perfection**. Also, Ōkubo Chōan, who led a group of ninja and mine brokers and made a huge fortune from developing gold-mines but was later assassinated, was also a prominent *Noh* actor. So perhaps they may also have been ninja.

Q Were mine brokers also ninja?

There was a surge in the output of gold mines and silver mines all over the country when **Toyotomi Hideyoshi came to power**. Behind him were professional mine brokers who served Ōkubo Chōan and other former Takeda family members whom we discussed above. The know-how for developing and refining precious metals was a secret. They moved from mountain to mountain all over Japan and developed a unique lifestyle and information network.

Legends ✈ 125

これまで農民の暮らし中心に研究してきた日本の歴史学も、やっと「**山の民**」「**海の民**」などに目を向けています。忍者や山伏のネットワークと重なっていることが明らかになる日も遠くないでしょう。

Q 俳諧の松尾芭蕉も忍者だった？

彼も出身は伊賀の柘植。ここも忍者の里です。彼の父・松尾与左衛門は**名字帯刀を許された**上層農民。母は伊賀の上級忍者・百地氏の娘。これだけでも忍者を束ねる家系の出身だとわかります。

俳諧や連歌の師匠も旅に出て怪しまれない職業だったこと。彼の旅行記『奥の細道』は、1日平均42kmという異常な速度での移動といい、**旅費の出所**が不明なことといい、謎だらけ。こうしたことから、幕府の**密命**を受けて諸藩の動きを探るためだったのではないかと言われています。

Q 「川中島の戦い」は忍者どうしの戦いだった？

何度も映画や小説やTVドラマにもなった「川中島の戦い」は、甲斐（山梨県）の武田信玄と越後（新潟県）の上杉謙信が、1553年から12年をかけて計5回も戦った戦争です。

Japanese historians have long focused on the lives of farmers, but they are now turning their attention toward **mountain folk and seafarers**. The day when they discover evidence that such people belonged to networks of ninja or mountain priests is close.

Q Was Matsuo Bashō a ninja?

Matsuo Bashō came from Tsuge, Iga, another hometown of ninja. His father Matsuo Yozaemon was an upper-class farmer who was **permitted to have a surname and wear a sword**. His mother was a daughter of the Momochi family. Momochi was a senior ninja, so we could infer that he was from a family of ninjas.

He was a master of *haiku* and verse linking, which is a profession that implies that he was not suspected when he was traveling. His travel essay *Oku no Hosomichi* (The Narrow Road to the Deep North) is full of mysteries because his average daily traveling distance was an extraordinary 42 km and it was not clear from where he got the **funds for his travels**. So some people say that he was in charge of spies on various domains under the **secret orders** of the Tokugawa Shogunate.

Q Were the Battles of Kawanakajima fought by ninja?

The Battles of Kawanakajima were fought between Takeda Shingen from the Kai region (Yamanashi Prefecture) and Uesugi Kenshin from the Echigo region (Niigata Prefecture). Five major battles were fought there over a period of 12 years starting in 1553, and the

とくに1561年、最大の激戦となった第四次戦争は、**千曲川と犀川が合流する三角地**である「川中島」で行われました。この時、武田は軍の一部を上杉の背後に回らせて自陣側に追い立てる「きつつき作戦」を用いようとしました。名参謀・山本勘助の提案でした。

　しかし、上杉勢の忍者（「軒猿」）がそれを察知して陣営はもぬけの殻に。敵の動きを直前まで探査して報告したはずの甲斐の忍者（「三つ者」）の敗北でした。

Q 「**風魔小太郎**」に興味があるので教えてください

　戦国時代における相模（神奈川県）の北条忍者の代表は、風魔あるいは風間の一族でした。風間は足柄郡にある地名です。その一族を率いていたのが風魔小太郎で、身長2.16mの大男。筋骨荒々しく毛むくじゃら、手にこぶがあり、眼や口が大きく裂けていて、牙のような歯が4本外に出ており、頭は福禄寿に似て鼻高しというのですから、まさに鬼のよう。

　彼は**山賊、海賊、強盗、窃盗**の計200人を束ね、

128 ✦ 伝説

Battles have been dramatized by movies, novels and TV dramas many times.

The fourth major battle in 1561 was the biggest conflict. It was fought on Kawanakajima, a **triangular area where the Chikuma River and Sai River merged**. At that time, the Takeda army tried to employ a "woodpecker strategy" to get some of the soldiers behind the Uesugi army to push the enemy into Takeda's territory. This was proposed by a great strategist on the military staff, Yamamoto Kansuke.

However, Uesugi's ninja (*nokizaru*) detected the plot beforehand and moved from their position. Ninja from the Kai region (*mitsumono*) should have spied on the enemy's movement until just before the tactics were deployed and duly reported it, but *nokizaru* got the better of them.

Q Tell me about Fūma Kotarō.

During the Age of the Warring States, the Fūma or Kazama family led Hōjō ninja in Sagami (Kanagawa Prefecture). Kazama is the name of a place in Asigara-gun, Kanagawa. Fūma Kotarō was the leader of the family, and was more than seven feet tall. He looked like a demon, powerfully built and hairy, lumps on his knuckles, eyes and mouth split broadly, four of his teeth sticking out like fangs, head resembling *Fukurokuju* (the God of Wealth and Longevity) and long-nosed.

He led a total of 200 **bandits**, **pirates**, **robbers**

Legends 129

敵陣に忍び込んでは捕虜を捕まえたり、繋がれた馬を放したり、放火するなどして大暴れしました。その末裔たちは平和になった江戸期に強盗集団になってしまい、ことごとく滅ぼされました。しばしば映画などで悪役に描かれるのは、この時期の、何代目かの風魔小太郎でしょう。

Q 「上忍・中忍・下忍」というのは忍者の階級ですか？

忍者組織は**厳格な命令系統**が必要だったので、ピラミッド型の階級組織を持っていたように伝えられますが、確実なことはわかりません。でも「上忍・中忍・下忍」という言葉はあります。これは階級の名前ではなく**忍者としての評価**でした。

「上忍」は、技術を持つが名前は知られていない者。その方が活動できる。「中忍」は技術もあり名前も知られている者、「下忍」は技術もなく名前も知られていない者。誰かに従属してその指示で行動します。

Q 昔の日本人は歩く時の形が違っていたのは本当ですが？

古武術のある研究者が、「江戸時代以前の日本人は、**右手と右足、左手と左足をそれぞれ同時に出して前に進む歩き方**をしていた。歌舞伎などではこれを"ナンバ歩き"と言う」という説を出しました。この応用が"ナンバ走り"で、**飛脚**が遠距離を驚異的な速度で走れた理由とされま

130 ✦ 伝説

and **thieves**, sneaking into the enemy's camp and capturing prisoners, letting loose subdued horses or setting fires. In the peaceful Edo period, his descendants became robbers and all were destroyed. It was a decscendant of Fūma Kotarō who often appeared as a villain in movies during that period.

Q Are *jōnin, chūnin* or *genin* ninja ranks?

Ninja groups needed a **rigorous chain of command**, so they reportedly had a pyramidal hierarchy, but this is by no means certain. However, the words *jōnin* (high-ranking ninja), *chūnin* (middle-ranking ninja) and *genin* (low-ranking ninja) have been handed down to us. However, these words represented the **evaluation of a ninja**, not their position.

Jōnin were skilled but their names were not public so they could engage in various activities easily. *Chūnin* were skilled and their names were public. *Genin*, who acted under the instruction of other people, were not skilled and their names were not public.

Q Did Japanese people walk differently in the past?

According to a researcher of Japanese traditional martial arts, Japanese people before the Edo period walked by **bringing forward the right hand and the right foot, and the left hand and the left foot**, alternately, which was called *namba aruki* (ninja walk) in Kabuki. He also argues that the same system of running called

す。そして忍者の走り方だったというのです。

最近の日本人ランナーにもこの走り方で好記録を出す人がいたと話題になりました。しかし、スポーツ科学的に見て合理的かどうか、本当にそんな歩き方したのかどうか、曖昧なところが多い学説です。

Q 東京の原宿、青山、赤坂は忍者の住む町だったのですか？

幕府は防衛のために要所に伊賀・甲賀の組屋敷や住宅地を置きました。彼らは与えられた**土地の開拓者でもありました。**

原宿、青山、赤坂の一ツ木、渋谷の隠田、四谷の旧町名にあった伊賀町、甲賀町などがそうです。郊外では練馬の大泉、三鷹の新川、狛江、調布などにも彼らの土地がありました。

Q 「猿飛佐助」は実在の人物ですか？

「猿飛佐助」は、子ども向け忍者物語や映画の大ヒーローであり、**真田幸村（信繁）に仕える**「真田十勇士」の一人として、霧隠才蔵や三好清海入道、穴山小助らと大活躍します。

架空の人物ですが、朽木谷の山賊だったのが秀吉配下になった猿飛仁助や、伊賀の下忍・下

132 ✦ 伝説

namba hashiri (ninja running) was the secret behind ancient **express messengers** running a long distance at an amazing pace and that ninja also adopted this.

More recently, a Japanese runner who employed this method and produced good records drew attention. However, this theory is rather questionable; it is uncertain whether it is rational in terms of sports science or whether they really walked that way.

Q Were Harajuku, Aoyama or Akasaka in Tokyo ninja towns?

For security reasons, the Tokugawa Shogunate offered *kumi-yashiki* (residences for general samurai) or houses of Iga and Kōga to ninja at important points, and **ninja cleared and the uncultivated land** given to them.

Such places included Harajuku, Aoyama, Hitotsugi in Akasaka, Onden in Shibuya, and the formerly called Iga-machi and Kōga-machi towns near Yotsuya. In the suburbs, their lands were in Ōizumi in Nerima, Shinkawa in Mitaka, Komae and Chōfu.

Q Was Sarutobi Sasuke a real character?

Sarutobi Sasuke was a great hero in ninja stories and movies for children who was active as one of the Sanada Ten Braves and **served Sanada Yukimura (Nobushige)** along with his colleagues Kirigakure Saizō, Miyoshi Seikainyūdō and Anayama Kosuke.

He is a fictional figure, but Sarutobi Nisuke, who was originally a bandit in Kutsukidani but later served

柘植ノ木猿の本名が上月佐助だったことから、彼こそ実在したモデルではないかとの説があります。

「猿飛」というのは、猿のように木の枝から枝と飛び移る身軽な体術を得意としていたからと言われます。

Q 少年マンガ『サスケ』のことも知りたい

白土三平が、少年雑誌に連載(1961年-1966年、全55話)、アニメ化もされました。

少年忍者「サスケ」の父は真田忍者。**色々なワザや現象**に合理的な説明や図解が付けられ、それが科学的かどうかは別にして、従来の、超人的な身体能力と幻術的なワザしか描かれなかった忍者ものとは違う知的な新鮮さを与えました。

白土は、以前に『忍者武芸帳』を発表し、『サスケ』以降は、『カムイ伝』、『カムイ外伝』などを発表しています。これらは、単に忍者を描くのでなく、**農民たちの反抗**や**戦乱に苦しむ庶民**など階級闘争的な視点から歴史全体を描いていると評価されました。

134 ✦ 伝説

Toyotomi Hideyoshi, or a low-ranking ninja of the Iga School, Shimotsuge no Kizaru (whose real name was Kōzuki Sasuke) may have been the actual inspiration for Sarutobi Sasuke.

Sarutobi (literally flying monkey) is so called because he was reportedly good at agile *taijutsu* (unarmed combat techniques) such as jumping from branch to branch like a monkey.

Q Please tell me about the boys' manga comic, *Sasuke*.

Shirato Sanpei published a manga serial in a boys' magazine (1961–1966, containing 55 anecdotes), and an anime was produced based on the manga.

The father of the boy ninja Sasuke is a Sanada ninja. Sirato gave reasonable explanations about and illustrations of **various skills and phenomena**, scientific or otherwise, which offered readers a unique intellectual freshness, as other ninja comics only described superhuman physical activities or illusionist skills.

Shirato published *Ninja Bugeichō* (Tales of the Ninja) before *Sasuke*, and after *Sasuke*, he drew *Kamui Den* (The Legend of Kamui), *Kamui Gaiden* (The Side Story of Kamui) and other works. These works were highly evaluated as they not only described ninja, but also depicted the entire history including **rebellious peasants** as well as **ordinary people suffering from war** from a perspective that was based on the history of class struggle.

Q TVのスポーツ系番組『SASUKE』と関係ありますか？

身軽に移動する体術を競うことから忍者「サスケ」のタイトルがついただけです。1997年から放送されたこの番組は、さまざまな障害物をクリアする**肉体系サバイバルゲーム**で、2017年までに33回放送されたうち、すべてクリアして賞金200万円を獲得できたのは3300人の中で4人だけです。

女性版SASUKEの「KUNOICHI」もあり、2006年10月からは全米でも『Ninja Warrior』という名前で放送されて大人気。2009年からは米国独自制作も開始。日本の番組で最多となる世界165の国と地域で放送されています。

Q 忍者のイメージを創ったTV番組『隠密剣士』って何？

1962年-1965年の間に計128話放映。江戸時代中期、将軍家斉の腹違いの兄・松平信千代が隠密・秋草新太郎（俳優：大瀬康一）に化け、**諸国を旅しながら、悪人の忍者集団と戦う物語**です。相棒は忍者「霧の遁兵衛」（同：牧冬吉）。**刀の柄を逆手に持つ構え**や、卍型手裏剣（star knives）、それを両手の平を水平に合わせた状態で連投する方法などは、このドラマで工夫され、後の忍者映画では皆、これを真似しました。

Q Is the comic *Sasuke* related to *SASUKE*, a sports program on TV?

The ninja-like title of the TV program *SASUKE* is so named just because participants compete in agile *taijutsu* (unarmed combat techniques). This program, which has been on TV since 1997, is a **physical survival game** where participants must get over various obstacles and cross the finish line. Thirty-three episodes have been broadcast, but there have been only four winners out of 3,300 participants who have achieved the goal and won the prize of two million yen.

KUNOICHI, a female-version of *SASUKE*, is also broadcast, and since October 2006 *SASUKE* episodes have been broadcast under the name of *Ninja Warrior* and become quite popular. American versions have been produced since 2009, and the series has been broadcast in a record-breaking 165 countries and regions,

Q Did *The Samurai*, a TV program help to establish the image of ninja?

The Samurai is a story about Matsudaira Nobuchiyo, a half-sibling of Shogun Tokugawa Ienari in the mid Edo period, who disguises himself as an *onmitsu*, Akikusa Shintarō (actor: Ōse Kōichi), **travels around Japan and fights against evil groups of ninja**. In total, 128 episodes were broadcast from 1962 to 1965. His partner was a ninja named Kirino Tonbei (actor: Maki Fuyukichi). The style of **holding a sword with a backward grip** and the method of throwing a *shuriken*

この番組は、『The SAMURAI』の題名で英語吹替え版が海外に輸出され、とくにオーストラリアでは、主人公「Shintaro」が大人気となり、主役の大瀬が1965年に訪問した際の歓迎ぶりはビートルズの時以上だと言われました。

Q 「児雷也」という忍者のヒーローのことを教えて

「児雷也」は、江戸時代に作られた講談や歌舞伎のヒーロー。**盗賊ながら庶民の味方で忍術を使いました。**彼の得意技は、巻物をくわえて印を結び、煙の中から**巨大なガマガエルになって**登場すること。妻は「なめくじ」の術を使う綱手、ライバルは大蛇の忍術を使う大蛇丸。

戦前に映画化された作品は**日本初の特撮映画。**大筋でこのキャラクター設定を引くアニメやゲームもたくさん生まれましたが、有名なのは、マンガやアニメで大ヒットした『NARUTO（ナルト）』でしょう。また、この物語の元々のモデルになっているのは、宋代の中国に実在した盗賊で、盗みに入った家に「（俺は）来ているぞ（自来也）」と書き残したそうです。彼は妖術は使い

138 ✈ 伝説

or throwing them successively by putting the hands together horizontally and sandwiching them between the palms, were contrived in this drama and later ninja movies all followed suit.

This program was dubbed into English and exported under the title of *THE SAMURAI*, and the protagonist Shintarō became very popular, especially in Australia. When the actor Ōse visited the country, he was reportedly welcomed more fervently than The Beatles.

Q Please tell me about the ninja hero, Jiraiya.

Jiraiya was a hero in storytelling or Kabuki performances of the Edo period. **Though he was a bandit, he took the side of ordinary people and used *ninjutsu*.** His signature move was to appear out of smoke **in the shape of a gigantic toad**, holding a scroll between his teeth and forming a special gesture with his hands. His wife Tsunade used the skills of "slugs" and his rival Orochimaru used the *ninjutsu* of a huge snake.

The movie produced on the basis of the story during the pre-war period was the **first special effects movie in Japan**. Then a lot of anime and games were produced that used almost the same character settings, and perhaps the most famous of these is *NARUTO*, a megahit both in manga and anime. The origin of the character in this story is an actual bandit who lived in ancient China during the Song

ません。

Q 「石川五右衛門」も架空のヒーローですか？

実在の盗賊で、1594年に京都三条河原で一子と共に**油で煮られて**処刑されました。歌舞伎に出てくる五右衛門は、大泥棒だが**義賊**だとして大人気。寺の山門の上に立ち、金襴のドテラに大きく盛った鬘、手には大キセルといういでたちで、「**絶景かな〜**」とうなる名セリフは庶民がみな知っていました。出生地に「伊賀生まれ」との説もあり、これを元に作家・司馬遼太郎は『梟の城』で、主人公葛籠重蔵のライバル風間五平こそ五右衛門だったという話にしました。

Q 現存するニンジャ「初見良明」のことを知りたい

初見良明は1931年千葉県生まれで、戸隠流忍術の34代目継承者であるほか、古武道など9つの流派の宗家（本家）でもある武術家です。

道場の「武神館」は千葉県野田市に本拠を置き、世界50か国に支部があって、各国の軍人や警察関係者など15万人が**入門**しています。FBIに招かれて**護身術**の指導をするなど、国内だけでなく海外での評価も高い人で、『いま忍者 この知的変身術』（潮文社）ほか著書もたくさんあります。

Dynasty and left the message "Jiraiya" (I came) whenever he broke into a house. He did not use witchcraft, though.

Q Was Ishikawa Goemon an imaginary hero?

He was an actual bandit who was executed in 1594 with his son by **being put into boiling oil**. In Kabuki, Goemon is popular as a **chivalrous robber**. Standing on top of the temple gate, in a padded kimono with gold brocade with an oversized wig on his head and a big pipe in his hand, he famously says "**What an amazing view!**" All the commoners knew this line. Some say he was born in Iga, and based on this belief a writer Shiba Ryōtarō created a story, *Fukurō no Shiro* (Owl's Castle) in which the rival of the protagonist Tsuzura Jūzō, Kazama Gohei, was actually Goemon.

Q I would like to know about a contemporary ninja, Hatsumi Masaaki.

Hatsumi Masaaki is a martial artist who was born in Chiba in 1931, and is the 34th successor of the Togakushi-ryū *ninjutsu* (Togakushi school of *ninjutsu*) and the head of another nine schools such as one for ancient Japanese martial arts.

His training hall Bujinkan (the Hall of the Divinely Inspired Warrior) is located in Noda City, Chiba. Its branches have been established in 50 countries and about 150,000 people **have become his disciples**, including military people and police officers. He is highly valued both at home and abroad, has been

Q イランには「くノ一」育成道場があるって本当？

　イランでは2万4000人もの人が「忍術道場」で学んでおり、そのうち約3500人が女性です。なかでも1989年にできた古い道場では、体術・棒術・手裏剣などを教えています。

Q 日本に「ニンジャの日」ができて祝日になったそうですが？

　祝日にはなっていませんが、2015年から2月22日が「忍者の日」になりました。2を「にん」と読めば「にん、にん、にん」です。

　この日は日本全国で忍者に関連するイベントが開催されるようになりました。始めたのは滋賀県甲賀市で、町の観光誘致促進のために、（一社）日本記念日協会に登録しました。その日、市役所では30名の職員が忍者のコスプレをして仕事をする様子を公開しています。

invited by the FBI to teach the **art of self-defense**, and has written *Ima Ninja—Kono Chiteki Henshin-Jutsu* (Modern Ninja—the Intellectual Metamorphosis Technique), published by Chōbun Publishing, and many other books.

Q Is it true that Iran has halls to train *kunoichi*?

In Iran, 24,000 people learn *ninjutsu* at *dōjō* (*ninjutsu* schools), 3,500 of whom are women. Among these *dōjō*, an old *dōjō* established in 1989 teaches *taijutsu* (unarmed combat techniques), *bōjutsu* (the art of using a stick) and *shuriken* skills.

Q I hear Japan has a national holiday to celebrate ninja.

Though not a national holiday, February 22 has been National Ninja Day since 2015. If you say "2" as "*nin*" in Japanese, the date can be read as "*nin, nin, nin,*" which can be associated with the word ninja.

Ninja-related events are held all over Japan on this day. The first event was organized by Kōka City, Shiga Prefecture, which registered the date with the Japan Anniversary Association to attract tourists in the city. The city hall has issued a publication about how its 30 staff members are clad in ninja costumes and do their work.

Q 「忍者居酒屋」に行ってみたいのですが？

　店の中が忍者屋敷のようになっていて、スタッフが忍者のコスプレでサービスしてくれる「忍者居酒屋」が各地にできています。東京の赤坂見附の「NINJA AKASAKA」、秋葉原「忍者カフェ」、千葉県・木更津市の「忍者居酒屋」、大阪市・千日前の「忍者屋敷」、熊本市の「忍者屋敷」……。飲食店業界は変化が激しいので行く前に自分でチェックしてください。

Q I would like to visit a ninja pub.

Ninja pubs can be found everywhere; their interior is like a ninja house, and the staff members wear ninja costumes and wait on tables. Some of them include Ninja Asakusa in Akasakamitsuke, Ninja Café in Akihabara, Ninja Pub in Kisarazu City, Chiba Prefecture, Ninja House in Sennichimae, Osaka City and Ninja House in Kumamoto City. The restaurant industry changes rapidly, so please do some research when you plan to visit one of them.

PART 6

研究
Studies

ニンジャを学べる資料や"聖地"
Information and Places to Visit

Q 忍者のことを学べる本にはどんなものがありますか？

　江戸時代になり様々な学問が普及するようになると、忍術書も体系的なまとまりを持ったものが現れるようになりました。

　中でも「**3大秘伝書**」と言われるのは、『忍秘伝』4巻（服部半蔵門下 1655年）と『萬川集海』22巻（藤林保武 1767年）、『正忍記』3巻（名取三十郎正澄 1681年）です。でも現代人が現物を読むのは困難。**手頃なものは**2017年に出た『忍者の兵法〜三大秘伝書を読む』（中島篤巳 角川ソフィア文庫）や、『忍者の歴史』（山田雄司 角川書店）、研究者が監修した図解ものなら『忍者』（川上仁一 日東書院）がおすすめ。本書でも大いに参考にさせてもらいました。

Q フィクションではどんなものが参考になりますか？

　1950年代末から1960年代に起きた忍者ブームをリードしたのは、司馬遼太郎『梟の城』『風神の門』、村山知義『忍びの者』、五味康祐『柳生武芸帖』、山田風太郎『甲賀忍法帖』『伊賀忍法帖』ほかのシリーズ、柴田錬三郎『赤い影法師』などでした。

Q Are there some books on ninja?

When ordinary people came to have access to knowledge of various academic fields in the Edo period, several books describing *ninjutsu* in a systematic way were published.

Among them, there are the so-called "**three great books of secrets**," which are the four-volume *Ninpiden* (written by a disciple of Hattori Hanzō, 1665), the 22-volume *Mansen Shūkai* (Fujibayashi Yasutake, 1767) and the three-volume *Shōninki* (written by Natori Sanjūro Masazumi, 1681). However, it is difficult for people nowadays to obtain and read them. **More accessible books** include *Ninja no Heihō: Sandai Hidensho o Yomu*" (Ninja' Tactics: Commentaries on the Three Books of Secrets; Nakajima Atsumi, Kadokawa Sophia Bunko), *Ninja no Rekishi* (The History of Ninja; Yamada Yūji, Kadokawa), and an illustrated book produced under the supervision of a researcher called *Ninja* (Kawakami Jin'ichi, Nittō Shoin). I referred to these works a lot when writing this book.

Q What fictional books are reliable sources?

Shiba Ryōtarō's *Fukurō no Shiro* (Owl's Castle) and *Fūjin no Mon* (The Gate of Wind God), Murayama Tomoyoshi's *Shinobi no Mono* (Ninja), Gomi Yasusuke's *Yagyū Bugeichō* (Yagyū Martial Arts Book), Yamada Fūtarō's *Kōga Ninpōchō* (Kouga Ninja Scrolls), *Iga Ninpōchō*" (Iga Ninja Scrolls) and other series, and Shibata

70年代には池波正太郎『夜の戦士』『真田太平記』があります。楠木正成のゲリラ戦などは、吉川英治『私本太平記』（四）が面白いです。これらの多くが映画やTVドラマになっています。

Q **忍者ものの代表的なマンガやアニメは何ですか？**

すでに紹介した白土三平『サスケ』『カムイ伝』『忍者武芸帳』『ワタリ』、横山光輝『伊賀の影丸』『仮面の忍者赤影』、藤子不二雄Ⓐ『忍者ハットリくん』、タツノコプロ『科学忍者隊ガッチャマン』、小山ゆう『あずみ』、尼子騒兵衛『忍たま乱太郎』、そして鎌谷悠希『隠の王』、せがわまさき『バジリスク』、岸本斉史『NARUTO』などがあります。

ゆでたまご『キン肉マン』の「ザ・ニンジャ」のように脇役になっているものはさらに多数あります。現在の忍者ブームは、これらのアニメ作品がリードしており海外にもファンを生んでいます。

Renzaburō's *Akai Kagebōshi* (Red Shadow Figure) led the ninja boom during the late 1950s and 1960s.

Then, in the 1970s, Ikenami Shōtarō's *Yoru no Senshi* (Nocturnal Warriors) and *Sanada Taiheiki* (Saga of the Sanada Clan) were popular. As for Kusunoki Masashige's guerrilla wars, Yoshikawa Eiji's *Shihon Taiheiki* (A Private Book on the Record of Great Peace) is interesting. Many of them have been made into movies and TV dramas.

Q What are representative manga and anime of ninja?

In addition to Shirato Sanpei's above-mentioned *Sasuke*, are his *Kamui Den* (The Legend of Kamui), *Ninja Bugeichō* (Tales of the Ninja) and *Watari*, Yokoyama Mitsuteru's *Iga no Kagemaru* (Kagemaru from Iga) *Kamen no Ninja Akakage* (Akakage, a Masked Ninja), Fujiko Fujio A's *Ninja Hattori Kun*, Tatsunoko Production's *Gatchaman*, Koyama Yū's *Azumi*, Amako Sōbei's *Nintama Rantarō* (Ninja Boy Rantarō), Kamatani Yūki's *Nabari no Ou* (King of Nabari), Segawa Masaki's *Basilisk—Kōga Ninpō chō* (Basilisk—Kouga Ninja Scrolls), and Kishimoto Masashi's *NARUTO* have been popular.

There are many more other works in which a ninja plays a supportive role, like The Ninja in Yudetamago's *Kinnikuman* (Muscle Man). These anime titles have led to the current ninja boom, and now there are a lot of ninja fans outside Japan.

Q アメリカ・コミックの『ニンジャ・タートルズ』とは何ですか？

バンダナをまいた忍者の亀（タートル）軍団がヒーローのマンガです。米国では1980年代から『デアデビル』、『ニンジャコマンドー』など、忍者を主人公にしたコミックが登場しています。実写の映画もたくさんあり、日系俳優ショー・コスギの『燃えよNINJA』はヒットしました。どれも日本人が考える**正統派の忍者**とはかなり違いますが、これもイメージの中の「Ninja」の一つとして、楽しみましょう。

Q **忍者体験**ができる施設やイベントを教えてください

三重県伊賀市の「伊賀流忍者博物館」は、宿泊やローカル鉄道とセットした「忍者パック」で行けます。**コスプレして手裏剣体験ができます。**

静岡県・裾野市の富士山２合目には本格的に道場修行ができる「忍術道場—忍びの掟—」があります。また富士山の反対側である山梨県・忍野には富士急行が運営する「忍野 しのびの里」があり、**忍者屋敷の食事処**もあります。

以下、東日本だけでも北海道・登別の「伊達時代村」、長野県・戸隠の「チビッ子忍者村」、群馬県・三日月村の「絡繰屋敷」、栃木県・日光の「日光江戸村」、東京都・お台場のレジャーランド「忍法からくり屋敷」……とにかくたくさんあるので自分で検索してください。

Q Please tell me about an American comic, *Teenage Mutant Ninja Turtles*.

The heroes of this comic are a turtle ninja corps with bandanas on their head. Since the 1980s, comics featuring ninja have been published one after another, like *Daredevil* and *Ninja Commando* in the USA. Numerous movies have been released, and a Japanese actor Shō Kosugi's "Enter the Ninja" became a blockbuster. All of these ninja are quite different from what Japanese people think of as **"authentic" ninja**, but let's enjoy this variety of imaginary ninja.

Q Please tell us about facilities or events at which we can experience ninja.

The Ninja Museum of Igaryū in Iga City, Mie Prefecture offers a Ninja Pack, with accommodation and local railway tickets included. **You can wear a ninja costume and try throwing shuriken** there.

At the second station of Mt. Fuji in Susono City, Shizuoka Prefecture, there is Ninjutsu Dōjō (a *ninjutsu* school) Shinobi no Okite, where you can take part in some serious training. On the opposite side of Mt. Fuji in Oshino, Yamanashi Prefecture is Oshino Shinobi no Sato which has a **ninja-house restaurant** on site.

In East Japan alone, there are numerous facilities like Date Jidaimura in Noboribetsu, Hokkaido, Kid's Ninja Village in Togakushi, Nagano Prefecture, Mikazukimura Karakuri Yashiki in Ōta City, Gunma Prefecture, Edo Wonderland in Nikkō, Tochigi Prefecture and a leisure facility Ninpō Karakuri House in

Studies ✦ 153

Q 忍者ゆかりの"聖地"を旅行してみたいのですが

現地に立ってみることで学ぶことは多いですね。伊賀上野観光協会のホームページには「忍者の実像にふれるスポット」として、**城跡や寺社、墓所**など10数か所を紹介し、体験旅行のメニューも載っています。ライバルの甲賀市観光協会も、**忍者が修行した場所やゆかりの寺**などを紹介しています。

『忍術の教科書 2』（笠間書院）には、伊賀の史跡を25、甲賀を15ほど選んでコンパクトに紹介しています。

Q 勉強した忍者の知識をテストしてみたい

甲賀では2008年から「甲賀忍者検定試験」を行っています。伊賀もやっていましたが今は中断。ただしその際の「教科書」と言われた2冊の『忍術の教科書』（伊賀忍者研究会編、笠間書院）は今も購入することができます。

甲賀の検定試験は、講演会のあと上級・中級・初級の3レベルに分かれて学科私見を行い、初級ではコスプレと手裏剣投げに参加すると加点され、合格者には認定証が渡されます。今までは甲賀市だけの開催でしたが、10回目の2017

Odaiba Tokyo. Check their websites for further details.

Q I'd like to make a pilgrimage to some sacred places.

You will learn a lot by visiting such places. The official website of Iga-Ueno Tourist Association lists more than a dozen sites like **castle remains, temples and tombs** as part of a "Ninja Experience" and offers several options for experience tours. Its rival, Kōka Tourist Association, also gives details of the **places where ninja trained and ninja-related temples** on their website.

Ninjutsu no Kyōkasho 2 (Ninjutsu textbook 2, Kasama Shoin) gives a brief introduction to 25 selected Iga historic sites and 15 Kōga historical landmarks.

Q How can I evaluate what I have studied about ninja?

Kōka City has been running the Kōka (Kōga) Ninja Test since 2008. Iga also offered a similar test but it is suspended now. However, the two-volume *Ninjutsu no Kyōkasho* (*Ninjutsu* Textbook; edited by Iga Ninja Kenkyū-kai (Iga ninja study group), Kasama Shoin) are designated as "official textbooks" and are still available.

The certificate test offered by Kōka is divided into three levels of academic tests (beginner, intermediate and advanced). At the beginner's level, participants can gain additional points by joining cosplay and throwing *shuriken*, and successful examinees are given

Studies ✤ 155

年10月には東京でも開催されました。

Q 大学で忍者を教えてくれるって本当ですか？

　国立大学の三重大学人文学部・人文社会科学研究科のことです。伊賀市、上野商工会議所と連携した活動をしており、企画イベントや毎月の公開講座を開催したり、国内外の忍者関係資料をデータベース化して公開する活動などを行なっています。また、東京・日本橋にある三重県ショップの「三重テラス」でも公開講座が開催されました。

a certificate. The test used to take place in Kōka City only, but in October 2017, the 10th test was also held in Tokyo.

Q Is it true that there is a university that teaches a course on ninja?

Yes, at Mie University in the Faculty of Humanities, Law and Economics. This national university works in collaboration with Iga City and the Ueno Chamber of Commerce and Industry, holding events and monthly open seminars, and is creating a database of ninja-related materials both at home and abroad that will be made publicly available. Also, Mie Terrace, a shop located in Nihonbashi, Tokyo that specializes in Mie products, held an open seminar on ninja.

English Conversational Ability Test
国際英語会話能力検定

● E-CATとは…
英語が話せるようになるための
テストです。インターネット
ベースで、30分であなたの発
話力をチェックします。

www.ecatexam.com

● iTEP®とは…
世界各国の企業、政府機関、アメリカの大学
300校以上が、英語能力判定テストとして採用。
オンラインによる90分のテストで文法、リー
ディング、リスニング、ライティング、スピー
キングの5技能をスコア化。iTEP®は、留学、就
職、海外赴任などに必要な、世界に通用する英
語力を総合的に評価する画期的なテストです。

www.itepexamjapan.com

［対訳ニッポン双書］
忍者まるごと事典
The Ninja FAQ100

2018年1月11日　第1刷発行

著　者　　土屋　晴仁

訳　者　　坂本真実子

発行者　　浦　晋亮

発行所　　IBCパブリッシング株式会社
　　　　　〒162-0804 東京都新宿区中里町29番3号 菱秀神楽坂ビル9F
　　　　　Tel. 03-3513-4511　Fax. 03-3513-4512
　　　　　www.ibcpub.co.jp

印刷所　　株式会社シナノパブリッシングプレス

© Haruhito Tsuchiya 2018
© IBC Publishing, Inc. 2018

Printed in Japan

落丁本・乱丁本は、小社宛にお送りください。送料小社負担にてお取り替えいたします。
本書の無断複写（コピー）は著作権法上での例外を除き禁じられています。

ISBN978-4-7946-0515-3